The CoinHub

An Ultimate Guide
to Selling U.S. Coins & Silver

BLAKE ALMA

CONTENTS

PREFACE

Welcome to a journey that twists the conventional path of numismatics into an adventurous narrative of passion, perseverance, and pixels. Imagine transforming the simple act of flipping coins into flipping the script on your life's direction. This isn't just any tale; it's my tale, Blake Alma, the once FedEx employee turned numismatic pioneer, and founder of CoinHub Media. At the tender age of 23, I ventured beyond the confines of traditional employment, driven by a passion ignited by my mother and fueled by the sheer will to redefine success within the coin collecting cosmos.

Why collect coins and sell them, you ask? Well, aside from the obvious thrill of discovering a piece of history in your palm or the sheer joy of deciphering tales from tails, it's the unbridled excitement of turning a hobby into a treasure trove of opportunities. It's about the moment you realize that the coins jingling in your pocket aren't just loose change; they're miniature gateways to a world brimming with history, art, and economics. A world where every coin tells a story, and every sale rewrites yours.

Here at CoinHub Media, nestled in the heart of Lebanon, Ohio—a place where numismatic passion and entrepreneurial spirit collide—we've embraced these tiny metallic storytellers as our muses. Our office, a sanctum of creativity and ambition, echoes with the wisdom of Proverbs 3:5-6 and the clinking of coins, each sound a testament to faith and the boundless possibilities within the coin market.

From my early days, juggling jobs at a gas station, a local park, and later, FedEx, to the groundbreaking moment I decided to channel my fervor for coins into CoinHub Media, it's been a wild ride. A ride through ups and downs, through doubts and discoveries, all leading to a crescendo of over $2 million in coin sales on the Whatnot app. Who would have thought that the young enthusiast, fueled by curiosity and guided by faith, would someday lead a digital empire dedicated to numismatics?

But why pen down this book, you might wonder? Because within these pages lies more than just strategies and insights into buying, selling, and collecting coins. This book is a beacon for the dreamers, the doers, and everyone in between, looking to carve their niche in the world of numismatics. It's a compilation of lessons learned, pitfalls dodged, and strategies honed from the furnace of real-world experience.

Building upon the narrative of passion and entrepreneurial spirit, this book isn't merely a continuation of my journey but a deep dive into the symbiosis of numismatics and personal growth. *The CoinHub: An Ultimate Guide to Coin Errors*, my first foray into numismatic authorship, not only cemented my place in the coin community as a best-selling author but also underscored the rich tapestry of knowledge and intrigue that coins offer. This book, like its predecessor, seeks to unravel the complexities of coin collecting and selling, albeit through a lens that magnifies both the technical acumen required and the sheer joy that comes from engaging with history one coin at a time.

My path from a FedEx employee to the helm of CoinHub Media, encapsulating the essence of modern numismatics, serves as a beacon for aspiring collectors and entrepreneurs. The transition wasn't merely a career change; it was a testament to following one's passion against the odds. The early days of CoinHub, marked by rapid growth and widespread engagement on platforms like TikTok and Instagram, were exhilarating. Yet, it was the decision to pause, reflect, and ultimately return with renewed vigor that defined the resilience of both CoinHub and myself.

We returned with a bang with our partnership with Whatnot Inc. in mid-2022. It marked a pivotal moment, propelling CoinHub into the live auction sphere and solidifying its place in the digital marketplace. This evolution from social media to industry mainstay wasn't just about growth; it was about creating a community—a collective bound by the love of coins and the stories they tell. We are now blessed with nearly 2 million followers across our social platforms.

Before adulthood, my journey was intertwined with the outdoors. The challenges and triumphs of my early career in outdoor media, from hosting "The Outdoor Experience" to grappling with the darker sides of public life, taught me invaluable lessons about resilience, faith, and the importance of community. These experiences, although distinct from my numismatic ventures, are woven into the fabric of my approach to business and life. They underscore the importance of navigating the ebb and flow of public life with grace and humility.

In my writings, particularly *An Outdoorsman's Heart* and *The Outdoorsman's Legacy*, I delve into the introspective journey of finding one's place in the world. These works reveal a side of me that is reflective, seeking solace and wisdom in both the tranquility of nature and the meticulous world of coin collecting. My recent move to study marketing and Bible at Pensacola Christian College is a continuation of this journey—a pursuit of knowledge that enriches both the mind and the soul.

As we embark on this exploration of advanced selling strategies, investment insights, and the nuances of the numismatic market, remember that this book is more than a guide. It's an invitation to journey alongside me as we navigate the complexities and joys of coin collecting. Through the pages of this book, we'll delve into not just the mechanics of the market but the spirit of curiosity, learning, and community that drives us all. Welcome to a narrative where each coin, each sale, and each chapter in our journey is a step towards not just financial success but personal fulfillment and growth.

So, whether you're a seasoned collector, a budding numismatist, or simply curious about the flicker of fascination that coins can ignite, this book is for you. Let's embark on this numismatic odyssey together, flipping through pages as we would coins, uncovering the value and stories they hold. And remember, in the world of coin collecting, every day is an opportunity to mint your legacy. Welcome to the ultimate guide to navigating the numismatic industry, humor in one hand and a magnifying glass in the other, as we explore the captivating realm where passion meets profit.

INTRODUCTION TO COIN COLLECTING

Imagine stumbling upon a time capsule, not buried in the dirt, but hidden in plain sight, jingling in your pocket. This is the essence of coin collecting, a journey through history one coin at a time, where every piece tells a story and every collection is a personal museum. I am Blake Alma, and I've turned this fascinating hobby into a thriving digital empire at CoinHub Media. This book isn't just about sharing my love for numismatics; it's a roadmap designed to guide you through the intricate dance of collecting, selling, and understanding coins. It's about transforming what might appear as mere metal into meaningful milestones.

But let's be honest, venturing into the world of coin collecting can sometimes feel like trying to decipher an ancient script without a Rosetta Stone. That's where I come in. From my early days as a FedEx employee to founding CoinHub Media in the heart of Lebanon, Ohio, my journey has been anything but ordinary. Driven by a passion kindled by my mother and fueled by an insatiable curiosity, I've navigated the numismatic cosmos to bring you insights that are as valuable as the coins we covet.

This book is a treasure trove of experiences and strategies, designed not just for seasoned collectors but for anyone intrigued by the flicker of fascination that coins can ignite. It's about seeing beyond the monetary value to the rich tapestry of history, art, and economics that each coin represents. Whether you're looking to dive deep into the world of numismatics or simply seeking to understand what makes collectors tick, this book promises a journey filled with discovery, insight, and, yes, a good dose of humor. Because let's face it, diving into the details of coin errors, mint marks, and auction tactics can be as thrilling as finding a rare coin in your change, but it helps if you can laugh along the way.

So, buckle up and prepare to embark on an odyssey that twists the conventional path of coin collecting into an adventurous narrative of passion, perseverance, and pixels. Through the pages of this book, we'll explore the captivating realm where passion meets profit, flipping through strategies and stories as easily as flipping coins. And remember, in the world of coin collecting, every coin has a story, and every story has the potential to inspire. Let's mint our legacy together, one coin at a time.

Coin Collecting

In the grand tapestry of hobbies, coin collecting occupies a unique crossroads where history, finance, and art converge. The act of collecting coins is not merely an exercise in accumulation; it's an intimate dialogue with the past and a strategic dance with the future. This segment dives into the why—the historical and financial significance of numismatics and the savvy world of silver investment.

Historical Significance

Coins are the storytellers of the ages. Each piece, from the ancient drachmas of Greece to the modern quarters of the United States, carries the marks of its era. They tell tales of economic shifts, political upheavals, cultural triumphs, and the everyday lives of people long gone. For historians and enthusiasts alike, coins offer a tangible connection to the past, a way to touch history and learn its lessons without the need for a time machine.

Moreover, coin collecting opens a window to the evolution of minting technologies and artistic expression. The craftsmanship found in coin designs reflects the technological capabilities, artistic trends, and societal values of their times. By collecting coins, we preserve this rich heritage, ensuring that future generations can learn from and appreciate the intricacies of our shared history.

Financial Significance

On the financial front, coin collecting and silver investment embody the principle of wealth preservation in tangible form. Coins, especially those made of precious metals like silver and gold, have inherent value that can withstand the fluctuations of paper currency and the ephemeral nature of digital assets. They are a hedge against inflation, a safeguard in times of economic uncertainty, and a portfolio diversifier.

Silver, in particular, offers a dual appeal. As an investment, it holds intrinsic value, often moving independently of stocks and bonds, thereby providing a cushion against market volatility. Its industrial demand, especially in areas like electronics, solar energy, and medical technologies, underpins its potential for growth. Investing in silver coins combines the protective aspect of precious metals with the collectible value that specific coins may acquire over time, whether through rarity, demand, or historical significance.

Why It Matters

Understanding the historical and financial importance of coin collecting and silver investment illuminates the depth of what might seem like a simple hobby. It's a form of stewardship, a way to safeguard pieces of history and secure a measure of financial stability through tangible assets. This practice teaches patience, research, and strategic thinking, skills that are invaluable in any endeavor.

As we delve deeper into the world of numismatics, remember that each coin in your collection is more than just a piece of metal—it's a piece of history, a work of art, and a building block of your financial future. This is why it matters, blending passion with pragmatism, and why the journey into coin collecting and silver investment is one rich with rewards, both tangible and intangible.

CHAPTER 1: UNDERSTANDING AMERICAN COINS

Introduction to American Coins

The journey through the world of American coins is a voyage across the fabric of the United States itself, encapsulating its rich history, cultural evolution, and the ingenious spirit of its people. American coins are not merely mediums of commerce; they are storytellers, bearing witness to the nation's trials and triumphs, innovations, and the ever-changing ethos of its society. This chapter aims to unfold these stories, guiding you through the intricacies of American coinage, its historical significance, and the treasure trove of knowledge and opportunity it presents to collectors, investors, and enthusiasts alike.

The Historical Tapestry

American coins offer a tangible connection to the past, a way to touch history itself. From the early days of colonial settlement through the birth of a nation and its subsequent growth into a global powerhouse, coins have played a pivotal role in the economic and cultural development of the United States. Each coin minted is a reflection of its era, designed with symbols and inscriptions that capture the values, aspirations, and achievements of the American people at that time. Understanding the history of these coins is essential for anyone looking to appreciate their full value and significance.

A Diverse Array of Coins

The United States Mint has produced a vast and varied array of coins over the centuries. This diversity includes everyday circulation coins, commemorative coins that celebrate significant people, events, and milestones in American history, and bullion coins that offer investors and collectors a tangible asset with intrinsic value. Each type of coin has its own story, design intricacies, and value factors, making the field of American coin collecting both vast and fascinating.

The Science and Art of Grading

Central to the world of coin collecting is the art and science of coin grading. The condition of a coin plays a crucial role in its value, and grading is the process by which the condition is evaluated and categorized. Professional grading services, such as the Professional Coin Grading Service (PCGS) and the Numismatic Guaranty Corporation (NGC), use a standardized scale to grade coins, ensuring consistency and trust in the collectibles market. Learning about grading and valuation is crucial for anyone involved in buying, selling, or collecting American coins. We will talk more about this later.

Why Collect American Coins?

Collecting American coins isn't just about hoarding shiny bits of metal or trying to find that rare quarter that's actually worth more than your morning coffee. Oh no, it's an epic quest filled with the highs of snagging a coin so rare it makes other collectors green with envy, and the lows of realizing you just spent your laundry money on a dime. It's for those who revel in the thrill of the hunt, dreaming of stumbling upon a coin so valuable, it could pay off your student loans (or at least a month of Netflix).

Then there are the investment gurus, who see beyond the mere metal to the potential fortunes hidden within. They're the ones who can bore you to tears at parties explaining the numismatic value of their latest acquisition, but hey, who's laughing when they're making bank on their coin collection?

And let's not forget the hobbyists, for whom coin collecting is the adult version of a treasure hunt. It's about the joy of discovery, the rush of learning something new, and the warm, fuzzy feeling of being part of a community that gets just as excited about old coins as you do. Because, at the end of the day, whether you're in it for the history, the money, or the sheer beauty of these metallic marvels, collecting American coins is about embarking on an adventure where every coin tells a story. So, grab your magnifying glass and join the club—just don't spend your rare finds on a vending machine snack!

Types of American Coins

The landscape of American coinage is rich and varied, offering a fascinating array of options for collectors, investors, and enthusiasts. Understanding the types of American coins is essential for anyone interested in the numismatic field, as each category serves a different purpose and carries its unique history and value. Let's explore the primary types of American coins that have been minted over the years.

Circulation Coins

Circulation coins are the most familiar type of coin, used daily by the American public for commerce. These coins are produced in vast quantities and include denominations such as pennies (1 cent), nickels (5 cents), dimes (10 cents), quarters (25 cents), half dollars (50 cents), and dollars. Over the years, the designs and compositions of these coins have evolved, reflecting changes in technology, economics, and societal values. Collectors often seek out older circulation coins, especially those made from precious metals or featuring rare designs.

Commemorative Coins

Commemorative coins are special-issue coins minted to honor significant people, places, events, or institutions in American history. These coins are typically produced in limited quantities and are not intended for general circulation. They are often minted in precious metals such as gold or silver and sold to collectors at a premium over their face value. Collecting commemorative coins is a way to celebrate the rich tapestry of American history and culture, with each coin telling its own story.

Bullion Coins

Bullion coins are minted primarily from gold, silver, platinum, or palladium and are purchased for their metal content rather than their face value. The United States Mint produces several series of bullion coins, including the American Eagle, the American Buffalo, and the America the Beautiful series. These coins appeal to investors and collectors alike, offering a tangible asset that combines the intrinsic value of precious metals with the aesthetic and historical appeal of coin design. Bullion coins are also available in various sizes, making them accessible to a wide range of collectors and investors.

Proof Coins

Proof coins are the highest quality of coins produced by the United States Mint. These coins are struck using specially treated dies and planchets (coin blanks), resulting in a highly polished and detailed finish. Proof coins are typically minted in limited quantities and are sold directly to collectors in protective packaging. While they can be found in various metals, proof coins are most commonly associated with precious metals, making them a coveted item for both collectors and investors.

Error Coins

Error coins are the result of mistakes made during the minting process, resulting in coins that deviate from their standard specifications. These variations can include off-center strikes, double strikes, wrong metal compositions, and more. Error coins are highly sought after by collectors due to their rarity and the unique insight they provide into the minting process. Each error coin is a one-of-a-kind anomaly, adding an element of intrigue and rarity to a collection. Our first coin guide is all about errors you can search for. The title of our book is *"The CoinHub: An Ultimate Guide to Coin Errors."*

Grading and Valuation of American Coins

Grading and valuation are the heartbeats of numismatics, offering a standard by which the condition and market value of coins are determined. This process involves a blend of art and science, requiring keen eyes, experience, and knowledge of historical and market trends.

Understanding Coin Grading

Coin grading is the process of evaluating the condition of a coin, essentially assigning it a quality level. The Sheldon Scale, ranging from 1 to 70, is the standard grading system used in the United States. This scale assesses a coin's condition, where 1 represents a barely identifiable coin, and 70 signifies a perfect coin with no post-production imperfections at 5x magnification.

Mint State (MS): Coins in uncirculated condition, with grades from 60 to 70. These coins show no signs of wear, though they may bear minting marks or slight imperfections.

About Uncirculated (AU): Coins with grades between 50 and 59 that have only a trace of wear on the highest points.

Fine (F), Very Fine (VF), and Extremely Fine (XF): These grades indicate coins that have been in circulation but retain most of their original details. The grades range from F12 to XF45.

Good (G), Very Good (VG), and About Good (AG): Lower grades for coins that show considerable wear, with the main features still being distinguishable.

Professional grading services such as the Professional Coin Grading Service (PCGS) and the Numismatic Guaranty Corporation (NGC) provide grading services, encapsulating coins in protective slabs with their grade and authentication.

Factors Influencing Valuation

The value of a coin is influenced by several factors beyond its grade. These include:

Rarity: The number of coins minted, and how many are known to exist today.

Demand: The current market interest in a particular coin or series.

Metal Content: The intrinsic value of the precious metal within the coin, relevant for bullion and some collectible coins.

Historical Significance: Coins associated with historical events or figures may carry a premium.

Provenance: The history of the coin's ownership, which can add to its appeal and value.

Navigating the Market

Diving into the world of grading and valuation in coin collecting is a bit like becoming a detective in a mystery novel where the clues are as tiny as a dime and the plot twists involve the sudden appearance of an old nickel. It's essential to crack the code of numismatic market, armed with your trusty grading services and a magnifying glass to spot those elusive mint marks and errors. Think of price guides, auctions, and sales data as your informants, whispering secrets about the market value of coins that could either make you the Sherlock Holmes of coin collecting or leave you wondering why you're knee-deep in pennies.

But here's the kicker: grading is more of an art form than a science. It's the numismatic world's version of judging a beauty contest where the contestants are all over 100 years old and the judges can't agree on whether wrinkles (or patina, in our case) add character. The market demand for these metallic beauties swings more wildly than a mood ring on a teenager, making valuation a thrilling roller coaster ride that could either take you to the moon or leave you clutching your coin album in despair.

Engaging with the numismatic community is like joining the cool kids' table in the cafeteria, but instead of trading gossip, you're swapping insights and advice on the latest coin trends. Coin clubs, shows, and online forums become your go-to for deciphering the enigmatic world of coins, where everyone speaks in code about MS-70s and proof coins.

For those brave souls who embark on the quest of collecting, investing in, or selling American coins, understanding grading and valuation is your Excalibur. It's what separates the novices from the knights of the numismatic round table, ensuring your endeavors in coin collecting are not only profitable but also downright enjoyable. So, polish your magnifying glass, and let's dive into the treasure chest that is coin collecting—just remember, in the end, it's all about having fun and maybe, just maybe, finding that one coin that'll make you feel like you've discovered El Dorado.

You Made it!

And so, we wrap up our introductory odyssey through the annals of American coinage, a journey that's taken us from the fledgling days of the republic, through the corridors of the United States Mint, and into the very heart of what makes a coin much more than just a piece of metal.

It's been a whirlwind tour through history, where coins aren't just currency but the storytellers of the nation's saga, capturing its identity, values, and key moments like snapshots in a family album.

Cracking the code on the types of American coins is like unlocking the first level of a game that only gets more intriguing from here. It lays down the red carpet into a world where the beauty of a coin can make your heart skip a beat, and understanding its grading and valuation is akin to learning the secret handshake of an exclusive club. This chapter has been your initiation into a society where history, diversity, and the condition of a coin are the trinity, guiding you through the maze of numismatics with the promise of treasure around every corner.

Armed with the insights and principles unearthed in these pages, you're now poised at the threshold of a greater adventure. This isn't just about collecting coins; it's about embarking on a quest for knowledge, beauty, and a connection to the very soul of America. Whether you're the seasoned collector with tales as numerous as your coins, a budding enthusiast with eyes wide at the vast horizon ahead, or the savvy investor looking to add a gleam of precious metal to your portfolio, the road through American coinage promises discovery, education, and a link to a tangible piece of the American dream.

As we turn the page, let the light of what we've learned here illuminate your path forward. May your journey through the world of numismatics be laden with finds as enriching as gold but more priceless in heritage. Here's to your adventure in American coinage—may it be as enduring and compelling as the coins themselves. Welcome to the fold, fellow traveler; the journey is just beginning.

CHAPTER 2: THE WORLD OF SILVER BULLION

Introduction to Silver Bullion

Jumping into the silver bullion bandwagon is like opening a treasure chest in the vast ocean of precious metals. Here, silver isn't just another shiny object to gawk at; it's a star with a storied past, a utility belt of economic prowess, and a cape of investment potential. Picture silver bullion—be it in the form of bars, coins, or those little rounds—as your financial superhero, fighting against the dark forces of economic uncertainty and offering you a solid, tangible way to store your wealth. This isn't the kind of hero that flies around in spandex; no, silver is the kind that has been kicking it old school as a medium of exchange and a store of value since the days when togas were all the rage.

In this chapter, we're not just going to talk about silver; we're going to unravel its mysteries. Think of it as a behind-the-scenes tour of your favorite superhero movie, where you get to see how the magic happens. We'll dive into the different avatars of silver bullion, decode its role in the investment universe, and hand out pro tips for those ready to bring silver into their financial or collectible arsenal. It's like getting a backstage pass to the silver show, understanding why it shines so bright in the investment spotlight, what makes its market price do the tango, and how to navigate the dance floor of buying, storing, and selling this illustrious metal.

Whether you're the kind of investor who's been around the block, a newcomer with eyes full of wonder, or just someone who stumbled into the world of precious metals out of sheer curiosity, this journey into silver bullion is set to arm you with the knowledge you need to engage with silver in its most gleaming, tangible form. So, buckle up, future silver aficionado, as we embark on this enlightening expedition. By the end, you'll not only appreciate silver's luster but also its lasting legacy and lucre in the world of precious metals. Welcome aboard the silver express—next stop, Bullionville!

What is Silver Bullion?

Silver bullion represents physical silver in various forms, primarily including bars, coins, and rounds. Each form serves a different purpose and appeals to different types of collectors and investors. Silver bars are valued for their substantial weight and purity, making them a favored choice for large-scale investment. Coins, on the other hand, hold a legal tender status in their country of origin and often carry a numismatic value beyond the metal content, attracting collectors with their designs and historical significance. Rounds resemble coins in appearance but do not hold legal tender status, offering a blend of collectability and metal value.

The Appeal of Silver

The appeal of silver bullion lies in its intrinsic value, historical role as currency, and its industrial demand. Silver's dual status as both an investment and industrial commodity makes it particularly interesting for those looking to diversify their portfolios. As a precious metal, silver has been a store of wealth and a hedge against inflation and economic uncertainty for centuries. Its tangible nature provides a sense of security that paper assets cannot match, making silver bullion a cornerstone for both seasoned and novice investors seeking stability in tangible assets.

CoinHub: Your Gateway to Silver Bullion

At CoinHub, we understand the allure and value of silver bullion. That's why we've made it our mission to offer a diverse range of silver bullion products through our live stream shop on Whatnot. Whether you're a first-time buyer or a seasoned collector, CoinHub provides a seamless and engaging way to expand your silver collection or investment portfolio. Recognizing the importance of a positive initial experience, we are excited to offer all new buyers a complimentary $15 gift card for their first purchase. This gift card can be used during our live stream events, making your first foray into silver bullion not only rewarding but also financially advantageous. Discover our offerings and take the first step in your silver bullion journey by visiting us at www. coinhubstore.com.

Investing in Silver

Investing in silver offers a multifaceted opportunity, combining aspects of wealth preservation, inflation hedge, and potential for capital growth. Silver's appeal to investors stems from its tangible value, historical performance, and its dual role in both the investment and industrial sectors. To fully appreciate the potential of silver as an investment, it's crucial to understand its market behavior, particularly the history of its spot price fluctuations.

A Brief History of Silver Prices

Silver prices have experienced significant volatility over the years, influenced by a variety of factors including economic policies, market demand, and global events. Two notable peaks in the history of silver prices offer insights into the metal's investment potential and the factors driving market fluctuations.

The 1970s Silver Boom: The late 1970s saw a dramatic surge in silver prices, culminating in a record high in January 1980. This boom was driven by several factors, including high inflation rates, geopolitical tensions, and a notable attempt by the Hunt brothers to corner the silver market. The Hunts' accumulation of silver led to a speculative frenzy, driving prices up from around $6 per ounce in early 1979 to a record peak of nearly $50 per ounce. This period exemplifies the impact of market speculation and economic conditions on silver prices, offering a cautionary tale about the risks associated with attempts to manipulate the market.

The 2011 Peak: Another significant moment in the history of silver occurred in April 2011, when prices briefly touched $49 per ounce, echoing the highs of the 1980s. This surge was attributed to a combination of factors, including a weakened US dollar, ongoing economic uncertainties following the 2008 financial crisis, and strong industrial demand. The 2011 peak underscores silver's role as a safe-haven asset during times of economic instability and its sensitivity to both investment and industrial demands.

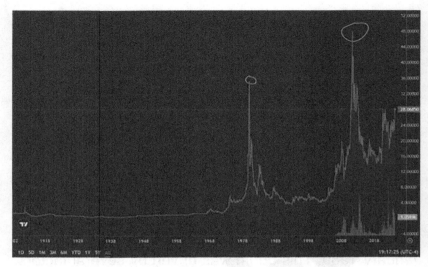

Silver Chart displaying the record highs.

The Impact of COVID-19 on Silver Prices

The onset of the COVID-19 pandemic in early 2020 sent shockwaves through global markets, leading to unprecedented volatility and uncertainty. As economies worldwide grappled with lockdowns, supply chain disruptions, and economic slowdowns, investors increasingly turned to precious metals as a hedge against inflation and currency devaluation. Silver, known for its affordability compared to gold and its industrial applications, became a focal point of interest.

Initial Impact on Silver Prices

Market Sell-Off: In the initial weeks following the global acknowledgment of the pandemic, silver prices experienced a significant drop, falling to below $12 per ounce in March 2020. This was a result of a widespread market sell-off, where liquidity concerns prompted investors to convert various assets into cash.

Industrial Demand Concerns: Silver's industrial demand, accounting for approximately half of its total demand, was also a contributing factor to its initial price drop. With factories shutting down and global economic activity grinding to a halt, the outlook for industrial consumption of silver darkened, further pressuring its price. **Risk Aversion:** The onset of the pandemic heightened risk aversion among investors, leading many to shy away from assets perceived as riskier, including commodities like silver, in favor of more liquid assets or those deemed safer, such as government bonds.

The Summer of 2020: A Record-Breaking Period

During the summer of 2020, silver prices soared, reaching heights not seen in several years. The price of silver briefly touched $29 per ounce in August, marking a significant increase from the lows experienced earlier in the year. This period highlighted the volatile nature of the silver market and the various factors that can influence its price.

Factors Contributing to the Summer of 2020 Silver Spike

1. Safe-Haven Demand: In times of economic uncertainty, precious metals traditionally perform well as investors seek to protect their wealth. Silver, often seen as a more accessible alternative to gold, attracted significant safe-haven demand, contributing to its price surge.

2. Industrial Demand Comeback: Despite the initial economic slowdown, the anticipation of recovery and stimulus measures led to speculation about increased industrial demand for silver, especially in areas such as renewable energy, electronics, and medical applications. Silver's dual appeal as both an investment and an industrial commodity helped fuel the price increase.

3. Supply Disruptions: The pandemic caused disruptions in silver mining and production, leading to concerns about short-term supply shortages. These supply constraints, coupled with rising demand, contributed to the upward pressure on prices.

4. Monetary Policy and Stimulus Measures: Global central banks' responses to the economic impact of COVID-19, including lowering interest rates and launching stimulus programs, weakened currencies and stoked fears of inflation, driving investors towards silver and other precious metals.

Lessons from the Silver Spike

The dramatic rise in silver prices during the summer of 2020 serves as a valuable lesson for investors in the importance of diversification, the impact of global events on commodity markets, and the potential for quick shifts in market sentiment. It also underscores the need for investors to stay informed and adaptable, ready to respond to changing market conditions.

The silver market's response to the COVID-19 pandemic, particularly the spike in the summer of 2020, offers critical insights into the complex interplay between economic events, investor sentiment, and commodity prices. For those interested in investing in silver, understanding these dynamics is crucial for navigating the market's ups and downs and making informed investment decisions.

Understanding Silver as an Investment

The historical fluctuations in silver prices highlight the metal's potential for both significant gains and volatility. As with any investment, understanding the underlying factors that influence silver prices is essential for making informed decisions. These include macroeconomic indicators, currency values, interest rates, and industrial demand, particularly from sectors such as electronics, solar energy, and healthcare.

Investing in silver can take several forms, including physical bullion, silver mining stocks, silver ETFs (Exchange-Traded Funds), and futures contracts. Each investment avenue offers different levels of exposure, risk, and involvement in the silver market. For those inclined towards tangible assets, physical silver provides a direct ownership experience. However, it also requires considerations for storage and insurance. Silver ETFs and stocks offer a more liquid and hassle-free investment option, though they come with their own set of risks and do not offer the same tangible ownership as physical bullion.

Navigating the Silver Market

For investors, the key to successful silver investing lies in diversification, research, and a long-term perspective. Understanding historical price movements provides valuable context, but it's also crucial to stay informed about current market trends and future outlooks. Monitoring economic indicators, industry developments, and geopolitical events can help investors anticipate market movements and make more strategic investment decisions.

Storing and Securing Silver Bullion

Once you've made the decision to invest in silver bullion, an essential consideration that follows is how to store and secure your investment effectively. The physical nature of silver bullion, whether in the form of bars, coins, or rounds, necessitates a thoughtful approach to storage. This ensures both the preservation of the metal's condition and the security of your investment. Here, we explore the various storage options available to silver investors, along with the advantages and precautions associated with each.

Home Storage

For many investors, home storage offers the convenience of easy access and personal control over their silver bullion. This can be achieved through the use of safes or secure storage areas within the home. When opting for home storage, it's crucial to invest in a high-quality safe that is both secure and offers protection from fire or water damage. Additionally, consider the placement of your safe in a discreet location to reduce the risk of theft. While home storage puts you in direct control of your silver, it also requires you to take full responsibility for its security and insurance, which can be a significant consideration.

Bank Safety Deposit Boxes

Renting a safety deposit box at a bank provides a secure off-site option for storing silver bullion. This method offers several benefits, including enhanced security features, privacy, and protection from natural disasters. However, access to your silver is limited to the bank's operating hours, and there may be size limitations depending on the size of the safety deposit box. Additionally, while safety deposit boxes are secure, they are typically not insured by the bank, meaning separate insurance for your silver may be necessary.

Precious Metals Depositories

For larger collections or investments in silver bullion, precious metals depositories offer a specialized storage solution. These facilities are specifically designed for the safe-keeping of precious metals and provide high-level security, including 24/7 monitoring, secure vaults, and insurance options. Depositories also offer the advantage of segregation, ensuring your silver is stored separately and can be easily liquidated or taken physical possession of when desired. While this option offers significant security and peace of mind, it comes with storage fees and requires trust in the depository's management and operational integrity.

Considering Insurance

Regardless of the storage method chosen, securing insurance for your silver bullion is a prudent step. Insurance provides financial protection against theft or loss, giving you peace of mind that your investment is covered. When insuring your silver, ensure that the policy specifically covers precious metals and understand the terms, including any deductibles or coverage limits.

Best Practices for Storing Silver Bullion

Diversify Your Storage: Just as diversification is wise for investment portfolios, diversifying your storage methods can mitigate risk. Consider using a combination of home storage for easily accessible pieces and secure off-site storage for the bulk of your collection.

Maintain Privacy: Be cautious about whom you inform of your silver bullion investments and storage locations. Privacy can be your best security measure.

Regularly Review Your Storage Plan: As your collection grows or market conditions change, reevaluate your storage solutions and insurance coverage to ensure they continue to meet your needs.

And that's a wrap on our thrilling expedition through the shimmering realm of silver bullion, where we've journeyed from the basics right up to the nitty-gritty of savvy investing, not to mention the adventures of storage and security. Think of this chapter as your treasure map, guiding you through silver's sparkling seas, marked with the highs and lows of its price changes—remember the rollercoaster ride of the 1970s and that breathtaking peak in 2011? It's all part of silver's charm, casting it as both a pirate's booty for collectors and a steadfast anchor for investors.

We've delved deep into the treasure chest, uncovering the jewels of how to invest, and the best ways to keep your silver safe and sound, like a true guardian of your own private hoard. As we close this treasure trove, it's clear that the lure of silver stretches far beyond its gleam, embodying centuries of history and holding the promise of a legacy that continues to captivate.

Whether you see it as a shield against the stormy seas of economic uncertainty, a sparkling addition to diversify your treasure trove, or a tangible relic of the planet's riches, silver bullion stands as a monument to the quest for value, security, and that deeply rooted human yearning to grasp a slice of the Earth's everlasting bounty. So, with our compass now set, and our silver in tow, we step forward—into the future, with pockets jingling and eyes bright, ready for whatever adventures await on the horizon of our precious metal journey.

CHAPTER 3: THE ART OF SELLING

Welcome aboard the "Sell Your Shiny Stuff Express," as we chug along into Chapter 3! Here, we're leaving the land of collecting and investing far behind and diving headfirst into the bustling marketplace. It's time to turn your treasure trove of American coins and silver bullion into cold, hard cash (or digital, whichever you prefer).

But hold your horses—or should I say, your coins? Selling these precious pieces isn't just about knowing what they're worth; it's an art form, a delicate dance in the grand ballroom of numismatics and bullion markets. This chapter is your backstage pass, your all-access guide to mastering the market's moves. From polishing your coins to perfection to picking the perfect platform to parade them on, we've got you covered.

Think of this as preparing for a grand debutante ball for your coins and bullion. You'll learn how to dress them up, show them off, and make sure they catch the eye of the right buyer. And let's not forget about mastering the art of negotiation—after all, it's all about making that grand exit with a heavier wallet.

Whether you're the seasoned collector whose cabinets are overflowing, the investor riding the wave of market peaks, or just someone looking to clear out some space, this chapter is your roadmap. It's packed with the tips and tricks you'll need to navigate the twists and turns of selling, ensuring you can part with your pieces confidently and profitably.

So, grab your gavel, or maybe just your mouse, as we embark on this journey from collector or investor to savvy seller. By the end of this chapter, you'll be ready to step into the market with swagger, armed with the knowledge to get the best bang for your buck—or rather, the best return on your relics. Let's get selling!

Preparing for Sale

The journey to selling American coins and silver bullion successfully begins long before the actual transaction. Preparation is key, involving a series of steps designed to ensure that your items are presented in the best possible light, thereby maximizing their appeal and potential value to buyers. This part of the chapter will guide you through these essential preparatory steps, from evaluating and grading your items to documenting their history and condition.

Evaluating and Grading Your Items

The first step in preparing for sale is to evaluate and, if necessary, professionally grade your coins and bullion. For coins, this might mean assessing their rarity, demand, and condition, as these factors significantly affect their market value. Grading, particularly by reputable services like the Professional Coin Grading Service (PCGS) or the Numismatic Guaranty Corporation (NGC), can add credibility and transparency to your sale, potentially increasing the buyer's willingness to pay a premium for certified quality.

For silver bullion, while the condition is less critical than for numismatic coins, the purity and weight are paramount. Ensure that bullion products are clearly marked with these details and consider having them assayed if their authenticity or metal content is in question. This can be particularly important for larger bars or less common items where provenance might affect value.

Documentation and Provenance

Documentation plays a crucial role in maximizing the appeal and value of your coins and bullion. For numismatic pieces, provenance, or the history of ownership, can significantly enhance value, especially for items with a storied past or connection to significant collections. Ensure that you have clear, detailed records of purchase, grading certificates, and any historical information available.

For both coins and bullion, high-quality photographs from multiple angles can provide a clear view of the item's condition and authenticity. These images are crucial for online sales and auctions, where buyers rely heavily on visual documentation to make purchasing decisions.

Setting a Realistic Price

Pricing your items appropriately is crucial for a successful sale. Research current market values, considering factors such as metal prices, numismatic premiums, and recent sales of similar items. Be realistic and aware that while you may have a particular attachment to your items, the market will dictate their value. Setting a price that is too high can deter potential buyers, while setting it too low may result in lost value.

Choosing the Right Venue

Selecting the appropriate venue for your sale is crucial. Different platforms and selling avenues cater to various types of buyers and have their own sets of advantages and challenges. Consider online marketplaces, auctions (both online and physical), coin shows, and local coin shops. Each option offers different exposure levels, fees, and audiences, impacting how you prepare and price your items.

By taking the time to properly prepare for the sale of your American coins and silver bullion, you position yourself for a more successful and rewarding selling experience. The effort put into evaluating, documenting, and pricing your items not only enhances their appeal to potential buyers but also ensures that you are well-informed and ready to navigate the sales process confidently.

In the next segment of Chapter 3, we delve into the various avenues available for selling coins and silver bullion, a critical step for anyone looking to convert their holdings into financial gains. Each platform offers its unique set of benefits and considerations, making it essential to choose the right channel based on your specific needs, preferences, and the items you're selling.

Places to Sell Coins and Silver

eBay

eBay is a global marketplace that offers vast exposure for your coins and silver bullion. It's particularly well-suited for sellers with rare, collectible items that might attract a higher price from a worldwide audience. However, the extensive reach comes with its challenges, such as significant competition, fees (including listing and final value fees), and the need for a strong seller reputation to stand out. Successful selling on eBay requires clear, detailed listings with high-quality photos and an understanding of the platform's policies and shipping logistics.

Whatnot

Whatnot provides a unique, live auction experience that allows sellers to engage directly with potential buyers in real-time. This platform is especially appealing for selling coins and silver bullion because it creates an interactive environment where sellers can highlight the unique attributes of their items, answer questions live, and build a community of repeat customers. The immediacy of live sales can lead to quick transactions, but it's important to build a following and understand the platform's fee structure.

Facebook Groups

Facebook groups dedicated to coin and bullion collectors offer a more targeted approach to selling. These communities can be very knowledgeable, providing a space to connect with enthusiasts who understand the value of your items. Selling through Facebook groups requires adherence to group rules and a personal approach to transactions. While there may be lower fees involved compared to other platforms, sellers must navigate payment and shipping arrangements directly with buyers, which can introduce risks without proper precautions.

Silver Wholesalers

Selling directly to silver wholesalers can be an efficient way to offload bullion, especially if you're dealing in bulk or less concerned about achieving maximum prices for rare collectibles. Wholesalers typically offer prices based on the current spot price of silver, minus a margin. This route offers quick transactions and reduced hassle but may not yield the highest returns for items with numismatic value above their metal content.

Other Internet Sites

Beyond eBay and Whatnot, there are specialized online marketplaces and forums for coin and bullion sales, such as Heritage Auctions or the Silver Stackers forum. These platforms cater to a more niche audience, potentially offering better prices for specific items. However, success on these sites often depends on having specialized knowledge and understanding of the community's dynamics.

Local Coin Shops

Selling to local coin shops presents the advantage of personal interaction and immediate transactions. It's a good option for those who prefer dealing face-to-face and want to avoid the uncertainties of online selling. Local shops can offer competitive prices for both bullion and collectible coins, but it's advisable to visit multiple shops to get the best offer. Building a relationship with shop owners can also lead to better deals and valuable advice.

Choosing the Right Platform

Selecting the right platform for selling your coins and silver bullion depends on several factors: the nature of your items (bullion vs. collectibles), your selling goals (maximizing profit vs. quick sale), and your personal preferences (online vs. in-person transactions). It's crucial to consider the fees, audience, and logistics associated with each option. Understanding the advantages and challenges of each platform will help you make informed decisions and navigate the selling process more effectively.

By carefully preparing your items for sale and choosing the most appropriate platform, you can enhance your chances of a successful and profitable transaction.

Selling Coins and Silver on Whatnot

Given our success at CoinHub that we have achieved on Whatnot, emphasizing the benefits and processes associated with selling coins and silver on this platform is essential. With over $2 million in sales in less than 2 years, our experience underscores the potential Whatnot holds for sellers in the numismatic and bullion markets. Here's a detailed look at selling coins and silver on Whatnot, incorporating insights and tips for leveraging this dynamic platform.

Whatnot is a live-stream auction platform that has rapidly gained popularity among collectors and sellers of coins and silver. Its live interactive format allows sellers to showcase their items in real-time, providing a detailed view and backstory for each piece. This direct engagement with potential buyers creates a dynamic and engaging shopping experience, encouraging immediate purchases and building a community around your brand.

Why Whatnot Stands Out

Live Interaction: The live format allows for immediate interaction with viewers, enabling sellers to answer questions, highlight specific details, and create a personalized shopping experience.

Dedicated Category: Whatnot has a dedicated category for coins and silver, attracting a concentrated audience of enthusiasts and collectors. This focused market segment increases the likelihood of sales and enables sellers to reach more potential buyers.

Community Building: Regular sellers on Whatnot, like CoinHub, can build a loyal following, fostering a sense of community and repeat business. This aspect is crucial for long-term success in the numismatic field.

CoinHub's Success on Whatnot

CoinHub's remarkable achievement of over $2 million in sales on Whatnot speaks volumes about the platform's potential. By selling under the handle @coinhub, we have not only capitalized on Whatnot's unique selling environment but also demonstrated the effectiveness of engaging directly with our audience. This success story serves as a compelling case study for the advantages of embracing live-stream selling for coins and silver.

Getting Started on Whatnot

For those looking to start selling their coin collection or silver bullion on Whatnot, the process is straightforward:

Sign Up: Interested sellers can begin by signing up at coinhubtv.com, a portal designed to streamline the entry into Whatnot's selling community.

Seller Application: Whatnot requires sellers to complete an application process, ensuring that the platform maintains a high standard of quality and authenticity. More information on this can be found at Whatnot's seller application FAQ and help articles.

Preparation: Successful selling on Whatnot involves more than just having valuable items; it requires preparation. This includes understanding the best practices for live sales, such as having clear lighting, detailed item descriptions, and engaging presentation skills.

Tips for Success on Whatnot

1. **Engagement:** Actively engage with your audience during live streams. Answer questions, share stories about the coins or bullion, and create interactive segments.
2. **Consistency:** Regular streaming schedules help in building a loyal viewer base. Consistency in quality and interaction encourages repeat customers.
3. **Promotion:** Utilize social media and Whatnot's built-in feature for live giveaways to promote upcoming streams, highlighting special items or deals to attract viewers.

Selling coins and silver on Whatnot offers a unique and lucrative opportunity for enthusiasts and professionals alike. CoinHub's success story is a testament to the platform's potential. By leveraging live interaction, focusing on a dedicated category, and building a community, sellers can achieve significant sales and grow their brand. Whether you're an established seller or new to the market, platforms like Whatnot open new avenues for reaching passionate collectors and investors in the numismatic and bullion fields.

Selling to Local Coin Shops

Selling coins and silver bullion to local coin shops represents a traditional and direct way to conduct transactions in the numismatic and precious metals market. This approach offers several benefits, including personal interaction, immediate payment, and the opportunity to build long-term relationships. However, there are essential aspects sellers should be aware of to ensure a successful and fair transaction. Here's a comprehensive look at selling to local coin shops and key considerations for sellers.

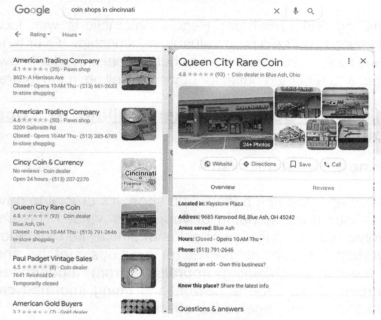

You can simply Google a coin shop near you.

Advantages of Selling to Local Coin Shops

Immediate Transactions: One of the primary benefits of selling to local coin shops is the immediacy of the transaction. Unlike online sales, which may involve shipping, inspections, and payment processing times, local shops typically offer on-the-spot evaluations and payments.

Personal Interaction: Dealing with local coin shop owners allows for direct communication and negotiation. This can be particularly beneficial for novice sellers who may seek advice or for those with rare or unique items that require special consideration.

No Shipping Risks: Selling to a local shop eliminates the risks associated with shipping valuable items, such as loss, damage, or insurance costs.

Building Relationships: Regular interactions with local coin shops can help build valuable relationships. Over time, these relationships can lead to better deals, insider knowledge, and a trusted outlet for buying or selling in the future.

Things to Consider When Selling to Local Coin Shops

1. Know Your Items' Value

Before approaching a local coin shop, it's crucial to have a realistic understanding of your items' value. This can involve researching recent sales of similar items, understanding the current market for precious metals, and, if necessary, obtaining appraisals from independent sources. Knowledge is power, and being informed can help ensure you receive fair offers.

2. Shop Around

Not all coin shops will offer the same prices for your items, as offers can be influenced by the shop's current inventory, demand, and the dealer's expertise in certain areas. Therefore, it's advisable to visit multiple shops to compare offers. This not only helps in securing the best deal but also provides insight into the market demand for your items.

3. Understand the Business Model

Local coin shops operate with overhead costs and profit margins, which means the offer you receive will often be below retail value. Understanding this business model can set realistic expectations for the transaction. Shops need to resell items at a profit, so their buying price must account for their business expenses and market fluctuations.

4. Negotiation is Possible

While coin shops have set margins, there's often room for negotiation, especially for rare items or large transactions. Being open to negotiation, armed with knowledge about your items' value, can lead to more favorable outcomes. However, it's essential to approach negotiations respectfully and with a willingness to find a mutually beneficial agreement.

5. Transaction Documentation

For significant transactions, reputable coin shops will provide documentation detailing the sale. This can include item descriptions, prices, and transaction dates. Such documentation is crucial for your records, especially for tax purposes or future valuations.

Selling to local coin shops is a viable and effective option for those looking to divest coins or silver bullion. It offers the immediacy of cash transactions, personal interaction, and the opportunity to foster valuable industry relationships. By entering these transactions informed and with realistic expectations, sellers can navigate the process smoothly and successfully. Remember, building a rapport with local dealers can open doors to future opportunities and provide a reliable foundation for your numismatic or bullion trading endeavors.

Selling on Social Media

Selling coins and silver bullion on social media platforms, such as Facebook groups and Instagram, has become an increasingly popular and viable option for many collectors and investors. This modern approach to selling offers a direct line to potential buyers, often resulting in quicker sales with lower fees compared to traditional online marketplaces. However, conducting transactions off-site using payment services like PayPal, CashApp, Venmo, Zelle, and even Apple Pay comes with its own set of considerations. Let's explore the nuances of selling through social media and how to navigate these transactions safely and effectively.

Posting a Sale on Facebook

Posting a coin for sale in a Facebook coin group can be an effective way to reach dedicated collectors and enthusiasts directly. When preparing your post, start with clear, high-resolution images of the coin from different angles, showcasing its condition, unique features, and any relevant markings. Accompany these images with a detailed description that includes the coin's denomination, year, mint mark, grade (if professionally graded), and any historical significance or interesting backstory. Be transparent about the coin's condition, noting any flaws or wear that might not be immediately apparent in the photos. Set a fair price based on current market values, considering both the coin's numismatic worth and its metal content, if applicable. Mention your preferred payment methods, highlighting if you're using services that offer buyer and seller protection. Let them know of the shipping cost of the coin too. (Note: if you offer free shipping, it will sell faster.) Lastly, encourage potential buyers to contact you directly for further details or to make an offer, and be ready to respond promptly to inquiries. This approach not only fosters trust but also stimulates engagement within the group, increasing the likelihood of a successful sale.

Search "coins" on Facebook, then switch to the groups tab.

Posting a Sale on Instagram

Posting a coin for sale on Instagram offers a visually driven platform to showcase your item to a broad audience of collectors and numismatic enthusiasts. To create an engaging post, begin with captivating, high-quality images of the coin. Utilize Instagram's multi-image feature to display various angles and close-ups, highlighting the coin's design, any distinguishing features, and its condition. In your caption, provide a concise yet informative description that includes the coin's denomination, year of issue, mint mark, and any relevant historical context or rarity factors. If the coin has been professionally graded, include this information to add credibility and appeal.

Incorporate relevant hashtags (#coins, #numismatics, #coincollecting, #silvercoin, for example) to ensure your post reaches those interested in coin collecting and investing. Engage with your followers by inviting questions and offers through comments or direct messages, indicating a sense of availability and openness.

For the transaction details, mention that interested buyers should DM (direct message) you for prices, payment methods, and shipping information. This direct line of communication can help maintain privacy and security for both parties involved. Encourage interaction by asking your followers to share their thoughts or tag fellow collectors who might be interested, increasing the post's visibility and potential reach.

Lastly, consider using Instagram Stories or live features to discuss the coin, its story, and the sale process in more detail, providing a personal touch that can enhance buyer interest and trust.

Advantages of Selling on Social Media

1. Direct Access to Interested Buyers

Facebook groups and Instagram accounts dedicated to coins and silver bullion attract a concentrated audience of enthusiasts and collectors. Selling within these communities allows for targeted marketing of your items to an audience that is already interested and knowledgeable.

2. Reduced Fees

One of the significant advantages of selling through social media is the reduction in fees. Unlike eBay or other online marketplaces that charge listing and final value fees, transactions conducted through direct payment services typically incur lower costs, allowing you to keep a larger portion of the sale price.

3. Personal Interaction

Social media selling allows for personal interaction with potential buyers. This can help build trust and rapport, which is particularly beneficial in the numismatic community where the story behind a coin or piece of bullion can add to its appeal.

Conducting Transactions Safely

Payment Services and Fees

When selling on social media, transactions are usually conducted through popular payment services like PayPal, CashApp, Venmo, Zelle, or Apple Pay. Each service has its own set of features, with some offering more protection to buyers and sellers than others. For instance, PayPal's Goods and Services option provides a level of safety by offering buyer and seller protection, including dispute resolution services. However, this comes with a fee (typically around 2.9% + $0.30 per transaction within the U.S.), which is a small price to pay for the added security and peace of mind it offers.

Importance of Using Goods and Services for Payment

Using the Goods and Services option when receiving payments through PayPal or similar features on other platforms is crucial for ensuring transaction safety. This not only protects you as a seller by documenting the transaction but also reassures buyers, making them more comfortable with the purchase. It's essential to factor in these fees when pricing your items to ensure you're satisfied with the net amount received after fees.

Communicate Clearly and Keep Records

Clear communication with buyers is vital, especially regarding payment terms, shipping details, and return policies. Keeping a detailed record of conversations, payment confirmations, and shipping tracking information can help resolve any disputes that may arise.

Shipping and Insurance

Once a sale is made, ensuring the item reaches the buyer safely is paramount. Use reliable shipping services with tracking and insurance, especially for high-value items. This not only protects your package but also provides a record of the transaction's completion, which is useful for both buyer and seller peace of mind.

Selling coins and silver bullion on social media platforms offers a unique set of advantages, including direct access to a targeted audience, reduced fees, and personal interaction. However, it requires careful consideration of the payment methods used, with a strong recommendation towards options that offer transaction protection, even if they come with a small fee. By following best practices for online sales, including using secure payment methods, clear communication, and proper shipping procedures, sellers can successfully navigate the world of social media sales, creating opportunities for profitable and safe transactions.

Legal and Tax Implications

The final section of Chapter 3 addresses an aspect of selling coins and silver bullion that is often overlooked but is of utmost importance: the legal and tax implications. Navigating the legalities and understanding the tax responsibilities are crucial for sellers to ensure compliance and avoid potential pitfalls. This section will outline the key considerations sellers should be aware of when engaging in the sale of coins and silver bullion.

Legal Considerations

When selling coins and silver bullion, it's important to be aware of and comply with any legal requirements that may apply. This includes adhering to laws related to consumer protection, which involve accurately describing and representing the items you're selling. Sellers must ensure that any claims about the rarity, condition, or value of a coin or bullion are truthful and can be substantiated.

For transactions that involve significant amounts of money, anti-money laundering (AML) regulations may also come into play. Sellers should be mindful of the thresholds that trigger reporting requirements and understand the need for due diligence in certain transactions. Keeping detailed records of sales and purchases is not only good practice for business management but also essential for compliance with AML regulations.

Tax Implications

Income Reporting

Revenue generated from the sale of coins and silver bullion is subject to tax and must be reported as income. How this income is taxed can depend on several factors, including whether the seller is considered a hobbyist or a business. The duration of ownership can also impact taxation; items held for over a year may qualify for long-term capital gains rates, which are typically lower than short-term rates.

Collectibles Tax Rate

It's important to note that the IRS categorizes precious metals, including silver bullion and certain coins, as collectibles. This categorization can affect the tax rate, with collectibles being subject to a higher maximum capital gains rate compared to other types of assets. Understanding how your items are classified and the associated tax rates is crucial for accurately reporting income and calculating tax liability.

Sales Tax

Sellers should also be cognizant of sales tax requirements. Depending on the location, selling coins and bullion may be subject to sales tax collection and remittance. The rules can vary significantly by state and locality, with some jurisdictions offering exemptions for certain types of precious metals transactions. Familiarizing yourself with the sales tax laws applicable to your sales is essential to ensure compliance.

Seeking Professional Advice

Given the complexities of legal and tax regulations surrounding the sale of coins and silver bullion, consulting with legal and tax professionals is highly recommended. These experts can provide advice tailored to your specific situation, helping you navigate the requirements and plan effectively for tax obligations.

The sale of coins and silver bullion involves not just an understanding of the market and sales strategies but also a thorough grasp of the legal and tax implications. By ensuring compliance with legal standards and accurately handling tax responsibilities, sellers can conduct their transactions with confidence and integrity. Keeping abreast of relevant laws and regulations, maintaining meticulous records, and seeking professional advice when necessary are all practices that contribute to a seller's success and peace of mind in the numismatic and bullion markets.

And just like that, we've reached the grand finale of Chapter 3, where we've unraveled the mysteries of transforming your cherished American coins and silver bullion into a successful sale. It's been a journey not just about finding someone willing to exchange cash for your collectibles, but about mastering the entire symphony of selling, from the opening note of preparation to the final crescendo of closing a deal.

This adventure has taken us through the labyrinth of online marketplaces, social media's buzzing bazaars, and the cozy confines of local coin shops, each path sprinkled with its own set of treasures and traps. The wisdom encapsulated in these pages is akin to a seasoned sailor's map, guiding you through the choppy seas of sales, ensuring you not only reach the shores of profit but do so with your integrity and legal standing intact.

Choosing where to cast your net—be it the vast oceans of online platforms like Whatnot, the bustling town squares of social media, or the trusted docks of local coin shops—can make all the difference. Each route is lined with its unique charm and challenges, from the siren call of wide audiences to the personal touch of face-to-face transactions.

Equipped with the strategies (more tips are in chapter 6) and insights from this chapter, you're not just setting sail blindly into the night; you're navigating with purpose, prepared to adjust your course as the market winds shift. Selling your coins and bullion becomes more than a transaction; it's an opportunity to weave your own story into the rich tapestry of the numismatic community, building bridges with fellow enthusiasts and collectors.

As we close the cover on Chapter 3, remember: the art of selling is a craft honed by patience, knowledge, and the courage to explore uncharted waters. With the compass of this guide in hand, you're ready to embark on your next adventure, charting a course toward fruitful exchanges, enriched connections, and, ultimately, a treasure trove of experiences in the world of coins and bullion. Bon voyage, and may your sales be as rewarding as the journey itself!

CHAPTER 4: AVOIDING PITFALLS

Welcome to the jungle of selling American coins and silver bullion, where the treasures are plentiful but so are the traps! This chapter is your trusty guide through the underbrush, aiming to arm you with the machete of knowledge to clear your path of common pitfalls and shield you from the quicksand of scams.

First up on our survival checklist is Scam Avoidance 101. Just as you wouldn't trust a map drawn on a napkin to find hidden treasure, don't take every buyer at face value. We'll dive into recognizing red flags, such as buyers who insist on odd payment methods or those who seem overly eager to close a deal without seeing the goods. It's like avoiding a pirate's handshake; if it feels fishy, it probably is!

Next, we'll navigate the tricky waters of market timing. Selling coins and bullion isn't just about what you sell but when. This section is like your weather forecast, helping you predict the best times to sell by reading the economic skies and steering clear of the stormy periods that could sink your profits.

Then, there's the art of managing expectations. Think of your coins and bullion as the crew of your ship; you need to know their strengths and weaknesses. Overestimating the value of your treasures can lead to disappointment, much like expecting a rookie sailor to navigate through a hurricane. We'll teach you how to set realistic goals and prepare for negotiations, ensuring you're not left marooned on the island of unsold items.

By charting a course through this chapter, you'll learn not only how to avoid the pitfalls that ensnare unwary sellers but also how to protect your precious cargo from pirates looking to plunder your profits. Whether you're a seasoned dealer or setting sail on your first selling voyage, these insights will help ensure that your journey is both rewarding and enjoyable.

So, buckle up your swashbuckling belt, hoist the sails, and let's embark on this adventure with eyes wide open. After all, forewarned is forearmed, and with the right knowledge and strategies at your disposal, you're set to navigate the bustling market of coins and bullion like a seasoned captain, ready to claim your rightful treasures while avoiding the siren calls of scams and pitfalls. Happy selling!

Common Mistakes in Selling American Coins and Silver Bullion

Navigating the sale of American coins and silver bullion is fraught with potential missteps that can undermine a seller's success. Awareness and understanding of these common mistakes are crucial for anyone looking to venture into the market. Here, we identify several key errors to avoid, providing sellers with the foresight needed to steer clear of these pitfalls.

1. Inadequate Research and Pricing

One of the most significant mistakes sellers make is not conducting thorough research on the value of their items before listing them for sale. This lack of due diligence can lead to setting prices that are either too high, deterring potential buyers, or too low, resulting in financial loss. Utilizing reputable resources, consulting with experts, and comparing similar listings are essential steps in accurately determining an item's market value.

2. Overlooking the Condition and Authenticity

Failing to accurately assess and disclose the condition of a coin or piece of bullion can lead to disputes and dissatisfaction from buyers. Additionally, not verifying the authenticity of items before selling can severely damage a seller's reputation and lead to legal complications. It's important to invest in proper grading and authentication from recognized services to ensure transparency and trust in transactions.

3. Ignoring Market Timing

Entering the market without consideration of current trends and timing can be detrimental. Sellers might rush to sell during a downturn or hold onto items too long, waiting for a peak that may not materialize as expected. Staying informed about market conditions and making strategic decisions based on thoughtful analysis rather than emotion or impatience can significantly impact success.

4. Neglecting Presentation and Marketing

Underestimating the importance of presentation and effective marketing is a common oversight. High-quality photographs, detailed descriptions, and professional listings can dramatically increase an item's appeal. Furthermore, choosing the right platform for the target audience but failing to market effectively can result in missed opportunities.

5. Overlooking Shipping and Handling

Improper shipping and handling practices can lead to items being damaged in transit, disputes with buyers, and potential returns. Secure packaging and choosing reliable shipping services with insurance and tracking capabilities are critical to ensuring that items reach buyers in their advertised condition.

6. Not Preparing for Legal and Tax Implications

Many sellers are unaware of or choose to ignore the legal and tax implications associated with selling coins and silver bullion. This negligence can lead to significant legal and financial repercussions. Understanding and complying with applicable laws, reporting income accurately, and consulting with professionals when necessary are indispensable practices for sellers.

By recognizing and avoiding these common mistakes, sellers can enhance their prospects for a successful and profitable selling experience. Thorough preparation, continuous learning, and strategic planning are key components of navigating the complex market of American coins and silver bullion. Keeping these pitfalls in mind, sellers can approach transactions with confidence, integrity, and the knowledge needed to achieve favorable outcomes.

Fraud Prevention in Selling American Coins and Silver Bullion

In the vibrant market of American coins and silver bullion, the potential for fraud is a significant concern for sellers. Ensuring the legitimacy of transactions and protecting oneself against deceptive practices are paramount. This section outlines strategies and measures sellers can implement to mitigate risks and safeguard their interests against fraud.

1. Verify Buyer Identity and Payment

Establishing the authenticity of a buyer's identity and the legitimacy of their payment method is the first line of defense against fraud. For online transactions, insist on using payment platforms that offer secure processing and protection against fraudulent chargebacks. Be wary of buyers who propose using unsecured payment methods or who rush the transaction without due diligence.

2. Use Trusted Selling Platforms

Selling through reputable platforms can significantly reduce the risk of fraud. These platforms often have built-in security features, such as user verification, secure payment processing, and dispute resolution services. Whether you choose online marketplaces, auction sites, or specialized numismatic forums, ensure they have a solid reputation and comprehensive policies for fraud prevention.

3. Document Everything

Maintain detailed records of all transactions, including communications with buyers, photographs of items sold, payment confirmations, and shipping documents. This documentation can be invaluable in the event of a dispute or if you need to report fraudulent activity. It serves as evidence to support your case and can help resolve issues more efficiently.

4. Implement Secure Shipping Practices

Shipping high-value coins and bullion requires careful consideration. Use insured and trackable shipping methods to ensure that items are protected from loss or damage during transit. Require a signature upon delivery to confirm receipt and consider taking photos or videos of the packing process to document the item's condition before shipment.

5. Educate Yourself on Common Scams

Familiarize yourself with the most common scams in the coin and bullion market. These can range from counterfeit money orders and checks to phishing attempts designed to steal your personal information or hack your accounts. Staying informed about the tactics used by scammers can help you spot red flags and avoid falling victim to their schemes.

6. Be Skeptical of Too-Good-to-Be-True Offers

Exercise caution if you receive offers that seem too good to be true, such as buyers willing to pay well above market value without seeing the item in person. These offers can be enticing but are often indicative of a scam. Trust your instincts and conduct thorough vetting of any suspicious offers. (Tip: This scam is very common on Craigslist; thus I don't recommend selling there.)

7. Seek Professional Advice

When in doubt, consult with professionals. This can include legal advisors, experienced sellers, or reputable coin and bullion dealers. Their expertise can provide guidance on best practices for fraud prevention and assist in evaluating the legitimacy of transactions.

Preventing fraud in the sale of American coins and silver bullion requires vigilance, knowledge, and the implementation of secure practices. By verifying buyer identities, utilizing trusted platforms, documenting transactions, and staying informed about common scams, sellers can significantly reduce their risk of falling prey to fraudulent activities. Remember, safeguarding your interests not only protects your financial well-being but also contributes to the integrity of the broader numismatic community.

Market Timing in Selling American Coins and Silver Bullion

Understanding and effectively navigating the timing of the market is a critical aspect of selling American coins and silver bullion successfully. The precious metals and numismatic markets can be highly volatile, influenced by a range of economic indicators, geopolitical events, and investor sentiment. Timing your sales to capitalize on favorable market conditions can significantly enhance your returns, but it requires insight, patience, and sometimes, a bit of luck. Here, we'll delve into strategies to help sellers make informed decisions about when to sell.

Recognizing Market Trends

Keeping a pulse on the broader economic environment and specific trends within the coin and bullion markets is essential. Factors such as inflation rates, currency fluctuations, and changes in interest rates can impact the value of precious metals. Additionally, collector demand for certain types of coins can vary based on numismatic interest, rarity, and historical significance. Regularly monitoring market news, subscribing to industry publications, and participating in numismatic forums can provide valuable insights into current trends and future outlooks.

Historical Highs and Lows

Understanding the historical performance of precious metals and specific coin types can offer guidance on potential future movements. For instance, recalling the significant spikes in silver prices in the late 1970s and again in 2011 can help sellers recognize patterns that might indicate a rising market. Similarly, being aware of periods of decline allows sellers to adjust their strategies accordingly, perhaps holding off on selling until the market rebounds.

Economic Indicators

Economic indicators such as stock market performance, the strength of the dollar, and geopolitical stability can influence investor behavior towards precious metals. Typically, in times of economic uncertainty or declining stock markets, investors may turn to gold and silver as safe-haven assets, driving up prices. Sellers should consider these broader economic signals when deciding the timing of their sales.

Supply and Demand Dynamics

The basic economic principle of supply and demand also plays a crucial role in timing the market. Limited supply or increased demand for specific coin types or bullion products can lead to higher prices. Sellers holding items in short supply or high demand might choose to sell during these peak periods to maximize returns.

Setting Realistic Expectations

While market timing can improve the likelihood of a successful sale, it's also important for sellers to set realistic expectations. The unpredictability of markets means that timing sales perfectly is challenging, if not impossible. Sellers should avoid the pitfall of perpetual waiting for the "perfect" moment, which may result in missed opportunities.

Diversification and Patience

A strategy of diversification and patience can mitigate the risks associated with market timing. By spreading sales over time and across different types of coins and bullion, sellers can take advantage of varying market conditions. Patience is key, as holding onto assets during down periods can often lead to better selling opportunities as market conditions improve.

Navigating the market timing for selling your American coins and silver bullion is like being a surfer waiting for the perfect wave. You need to understand the ocean (the market), watch the weather (economic indicators), and, most importantly, know your surfboard (the intrinsic value of what you're selling). It's a blend of art, science, and a little bit of magic that, while not foolproof, can lead you to ride the crest of profitability with style.

Staying informed is your compass in this journey. It means keeping an eye on market trends, just like a captain watches the stars, and tuning into economic indicators as if they were the wind guiding your sail. This knowledge doesn't just come; it's cultivated with patience and a keen sense of observation, allowing you to spot the undercurrents that could turn into the big waves of opportunity.

Patience, in this context, is more than a virtue—it's your strategy. Like a wise old fisherman waiting for the big catch, you know that jumping too early could scare away your prize. The market has its ebbs and flows, and recognizing the right moment to sell requires a calm demeanor and the ability to wait for the stars to align.

Combining these elements—the knowledge of trends, the insight into economic indicators, and the intrinsic value of your treasures—sets the stage for a successful sale. It's like assembling a puzzle where each piece is crucial, and when they fit together, the picture of profitability emerges.

Embracing the nuances of market timing, armed with information and patience, opens the door to rewarding outcomes. It's about not just selling, but selling smartly. Each coin, each bullion piece, holds a story, and by understanding the rhythm of the market, you become not just a seller but a storyteller, weaving tales that attract buyers at just the right moment.

So, as you stand ready, watching the market's waves, remember: the art of timing is your key to turning the precious metals and history in your hands into a successful venture. Let the dance with the market begin, with your eyes on the horizon and your strategy firm in hand, ready to catch the perfect wave of opportunity.

CHAPTER 5: ADVANCED STRATEGIES

Welcome to the major leagues of coin and silver bullion selling! Chapter 5 is where we go from playing in the minors to stepping up to the plate in the big games. This isn't just about selling anymore; it's about becoming a maestro in the orchestra of the numismatic market, where every move you make and every strategy you employ can turn the simple act of selling into an art form.

For the seasoned veterans ready to push the boundaries, it's time to look beyond the horizon and harness the power of relationships within the numismatic community. Think of it as networking, but instead of exchanging business cards, you're trading stories, insights, and perhaps even a rare coin or two. These relationships can be your goldmine, offering exclusive opportunities, insider knowledge, and partnerships that can elevate your game.

Diversification is your next secret weapon. Just as a wise investor spreads their risks across different stocks, a savvy seller diversifies their portfolio. This isn't just about having a variety of coins and bullion; it's about understanding different market segments and tapping into them. Whether it's branching into international coins, exploring emerging markets, or even venturing into related collectibles, diversification can open new doors and buffer against market fluctuations.

Then, there's the skill of staying ahead of the curve. In a world where trends can change as quickly as the wind, being able to predict or even set the next big thing can set you apart from the crowd. This requires not just knowledge, but intuition, a bit of daring, and an unquenchable curiosity about the market, technology, and the collectors themselves.

Chapter 5 is your advanced playbook, offering not just strategies but a mindset shift. Here, selling becomes more than transactions; it's about positioning yourself as a leader, an influencer, and a respected figure in the numismatic world. By leveraging relationships, diversifying your approach, and staying ahead of trends, you're not just participating in the market—you're shaping it.

Armed with these advanced insights, the world of coin and bullion trading isn't just a marketplace; it's your stage. And as you employ these nuanced tactics, remember: the goal isn't just to succeed but to thrive, turning every sale into a stepping stone towards becoming a legend in the dynamic and ever-evolving narrative of numismatics.

Building Relationships in the Numismatic Community

In the nuanced world of numismatic trading and silver bullion sales, the importance of building and maintaining strong relationships cannot be overstated. These connections can significantly influence your success, providing access to exclusive deals, insider knowledge, and a supportive network. This section delves into the art of relationship-building within the numismatic community, offering strategies to cultivate lasting partnerships with collectors, dealers, and industry experts.

Engage with Local Coin Clubs and Associations

Active participation in local coin clubs and national associations offers a fertile ground for nurturing relationships. These platforms allow for face-to-face interactions with fellow enthusiasts and professionals who share your passion. Attendance at meetings, seminars, and social events facilitates the exchange of knowledge, experiences, and contacts, laying the foundation for meaningful relationships.

Utilize Social Media and Online Forums

In today's digital age, social media platforms and online forums are invaluable tools for connecting with the numismatic community worldwide. Engaging in discussions, sharing insights, and offering assistance on platforms like Instagram, Twitter (now called X), and specialized forums can help you build a reputation as a knowledgeable and trustworthy seller. These interactions can lead to direct sales opportunities and partnerships.

Attend Trade Shows and Auctions

Trade shows, auctions, and conventions are critical venues for networking within the numismatic and bullion markets. These events provide a chance to meet a wide range of industry participants, from casual collectors to serious investors and renowned dealers. Making a positive impression through genuine interactions and sharing your expertise can open doors to collaborative ventures and exclusive offers.

Offer Consistent Value and Service

Building relationships is not just about making acquaintances; it's about demonstrating value and reliability.

Whether through fair pricing, exceptional service, or sharing valuable market insights, consistently meeting or exceeding expectations establishes trust and loyalty. Satisfied customers and peers are more likely to refer others to you, expanding your network through positive word-of-mouth.

Foster Transparency and Integrity

Trust is the cornerstone of any relationship, especially in a market as detail-oriented and value-driven as numismatics. Transparency in every transaction, clear communication, and adherence to ethical standards are paramount. Acknowledging mistakes, providing accurate product descriptions, and ensuring complete honesty in dealings reinforces your credibility.

Collaborate and Support Others

Viewing relationships as mutually beneficial collaborations rather than competitive encounters can lead to greater opportunities for all involved. Supporting fellow collectors, sharing leads, and offering assistance on projects can strengthen your connections and enhance your standing in the community. Collaboration can also lead to joint ventures, shared booths at shows, or collective buying opportunities, further enriching your numismatic endeavors.

In the intricate tapestry of the numismatic world, building and nurturing relationships is as crucial as the coins and bullion we trade. The connections forged within this community can provide not just transactional benefits but also a sense of belonging and shared purpose. By engaging genuinely, offering value, and conducting oneself with integrity, one can establish a network of relationships that enhance both personal and professional growth in the fascinating realm of coin and silver bullion trading.

Portfolio Diversification in Selling American Coins and Silver Bullion

Portfolio diversification is a cornerstone strategy not just in general investing but also in the specific arena of selling American coins and silver bullion. Diversification involves spreading your investments across various types of assets to reduce risk and capitalize on different market opportunities. In the context of numismatics and precious metals, diversification can protect sellers from market volatility, enhance overall portfolio value, and open new avenues for sales. Let's explore how diversification can be effectively implemented in your strategy for selling coins and bullion.

Diversify Across Metal Types

While silver and gold are the most popular choices for bullion investors, expanding into platinum and palladium can offer additional opportunities. Each metal responds differently to market pressures, economic indicators, and industrial demand, which means that when gold and silver prices are low, platinum or palladium might perform better, and vice versa.

Include a Range of Coin Types

Incorporating a variety of coin types, such as bullion coins, numismatic collectibles, and semi-numismatic coins, can also provide stability and potential growth. Numismatic coins, valued for their rarity, historical significance, and condition, often hold their worth independently of metal prices, offering a buffer against market fluctuations in precious metals. Meanwhile, bullion coins, tied more directly to metal prices, can offer quick liquidity and easier valuation.

Geographic Diversification

Exploring coins and bullion from different countries can expose you to new markets and demand dynamics. International coins, such as the Canadian Maple Leaf, the Australian Kangaroo, or the South African Krugerrand, can appeal to a wide range of collectors and investors. This not only diversifies your portfolio but also broadens your potential customer base.

Time Diversification

Time diversification involves acquiring and selling items across different periods, reflecting short-term, medium-term, and long-term investment strategies. Some coins and bullion might be ripe for selling in the short term due to current market trends, while others may gain significantly more value if held over a longer period. Balancing your portfolio with assets targeted for different time horizons can maximize returns and provide regular income.

Embrace Emerging Trends

Staying informed about emerging trends in the coin and bullion market can lead to early investments in areas poised for growth. This could include new mint releases, thematic collectibles, or burgeoning markets for lesser-known precious metals. Being at the forefront of these trends allows you to diversify into areas with high growth potential before they become mainstream.

Diversification and Risk Management

Ultimately, the goal of diversification is to manage risk and enhance the potential for profit. By spreading your investments across various categories, you mitigate the impact of any single market event on your overall portfolio. It's important to regularly review and adjust your portfolio to maintain a balanced approach that aligns with your selling goals and market conditions.

Portfolio diversification in the realm of American coins and silver bullion is a sophisticated strategy that requires insight, research, and ongoing management. By incorporating a broad spectrum of metals, coin types, geographic origins, and embracing new trends, you can build a resilient and dynamic portfolio. This approach not only safeguards against market volatility but also positions you to take advantage of diverse opportunities, ultimately leading to a more successful and sustainable selling practice.

Future Trends in the American Coins and Silver Bullion Market

As we delve deeper into the nuances of selling American coins and silver bullion, understanding and anticipating future trends becomes a pivotal strategy for advanced sellers. The market for precious metals and numismatics is influenced by a confluence of global economic factors, technological advancements, and shifting collector interests. Identifying these emerging trends can position sellers to adapt and thrive in an evolving marketplace. Let's explore some potential future trends that could shape the landscape of coin and bullion trading.

The Rise of Digital Platforms and Blockchain Technology

The increasing digitization of the marketplace is a trend that shows no signs of slowing down. Online auctions, virtual coin shows (like on Whatnot), and social media sales platforms are becoming the norm, offering sellers access to a global audience. Additionally, blockchain technology is beginning to make its mark on the numismatic world, with the potential to revolutionize how we authenticate, track, and transfer ownership of coins and bullion. Sellers who embrace these digital tools and platforms can enhance their reach and efficiency.

Sustainable and Ethical Collecting

As awareness around environmental and ethical issues grows, collectors and investors are beginning to place value on sustainably sourced and ethically produced coins and bullion. This trend could lead to increased demand for items with verifiable ethical credentials or from mints and producers committed to sustainable practices. Sellers attuned to this shift can cater to this emerging segment by highlighting the provenance and ethical considerations of their offerings.

Thematic Collecting

Thematic collecting, focusing on specific themes, events, or historical periods, is gaining traction. This approach allows collectors to tell a story through their collections, adding a personal touch that goes beyond mere investment. Popular themes include space exploration, significant historical anniversaries, and natural wonders. Sellers who curate their collections to align with popular or emerging themes can capture the interest of niche collectors.

Younger Collectors Entering the Market

The demographics of the coin and bullion market are evolving, with younger collectors beginning to make their mark. This new generation of collectors is tech-savvy, values sustainability, and may have different interests and collecting habits than traditional collectors. Engaging with these younger collectors through social media, offering educational content, and adapting to their preferences can open up new opportunities for sellers.

Integration of Precious Metals with Technology

The use of precious metals in technology, particularly in electronics and renewable energy sectors, continues to grow. As demand from these industries increases, it could influence the market value and investment appeal of certain types of bullion. Sellers should stay informed about industrial trends and consider how shifts in demand could impact their selling strategies.

Riding the wave of future trends in the American coins and silver bullion market is akin to being a time traveler, armed with knowledge of the past and a keen eye on the horizon. To not just survive but thrive in this evolving landscape, sellers must become chameleons, adapting with agility and innovation. Here's how you can harness these future currents to carve out success.

Leveraging Digital Advancements

The digital realm is your oyster, offering a treasure trove of tools and platforms to showcase your coins and bullion. Embrace cutting-edge technologies like augmented reality to provide virtual hands-on experiences, or utilize blockchain for secure and transparent transactions. Social media and online marketplaces continue to be golden avenues for reaching a global audience, but consider diving deeper into niche forums and platforms where the true enthusiasts gather.

Catering to Ethical and Thematic Collecting Preferences

The tide is turning towards more conscious collecting, where the backstory of a coin or bullion piece, including its ethical sourcing and historical significance, plays a crucial role. Tap into themes that resonate with societal shifts, such as sustainability and historical milestones. By aligning with these values, you not only appeal to a broader audience but also foster a deeper connection with your buyers.

Engaging Younger Collectors

The future of the market rests in the hands of the next generation. Engage them by speaking their language— think interactive content, gamification, and leveraging influencers within the numismatic community. Offer educational resources that are as entertaining as they are informative, making the world of coins and silver bullion accessible and appealing to a younger demographic.

Understanding the Industrial Applications of Precious Metals

Silver bullion, in particular, holds a dual allure as both a collectible and an industrial commodity. With advancements in technology and renewable energy, the demand for silver in industrial applications is poised to grow. Stay informed about these trends, as they can significantly impact market dynamics and pricing. Positioning your sales strategy to highlight these aspects can attract investors looking to diversify beyond traditional numismatics.

Anticipating and adapting to these trends isn't just about keeping pace; it's about setting the stage for a more vibrant, inclusive, and dynamic numismatic community. By leveraging digital advancements, catering to new collecting preferences, engaging the youth, and tapping into the industrial demand for precious metals, you position yourself as a forward-thinking seller in a market ripe with opportunity.

Embracing change is the key to unlocking future success in the American coins and silver bullion market. With a blend of tradition and innovation, you can chart a course that not only enhances your selling strategies but also contributes to the enrichment and expansion of the numismatic community at large.

CHAPTER 6: SELLING STRATEGIES AND SELLING TIPS FOR COINS

Navigating the wild world of coin selling isn't just about having a love for shiny things or a stash of coins that could rival Scrooge McDuck's vault; it's an adventure that requires a mix of Indiana Jones's courage, Sherlock Holmes's keen observation, and a dash of Gordon Ramsay's strategic planning (minus the shouting, hopefully. Garrett, I'm talking to you). Whether you're a seasoned collector whose home resembles a coin museum or a hobbyist looking to turn your pocket change into actual change, mastering the art of selling coins is more art than science.

Imagine you're preparing for a coin-selling expedition. First, you'll need your explorer's hat and a map—because diving into the coin market without a plan is like trying to navigate the Amazon with a blindfold. You'll encounter wild beasts (aka market fluctuations), quicksand (the pitfalls of poor timing), and maybe even a hidden treasure or two (those rare finds that can make the journey oh-so-worthwhile).

But fear not, intrepid adventurer, for you have a secret weapon: a treasure trove of industry knowledge and personal experience, gleaned from the legends who've navigated these treacherous waters before you. Armed with these insights, you'll learn to dance around the pitfalls with the grace of a ballet dancer dodging stage props.

Here are some gems you might uncover along the way:

The "Rare Coin Ritual": Perform this sacred dance to attract serious buyers (note: actual dancing not required, but highly entertaining).

The "Price Tag Tango": Mastering the art of pricing is a dance in itself. Too high, and you'll scare away the crowd. Too low, and you'll be crying into your coin folders.

The "Condition Conundrum": Discover why sometimes looking old and worn is actually a good thing (unfortunately, only applies to coins).

By the end of this expedition, you'll not only have transformed from a coin-collecting novice to a savvy seller, but you might also have enough tales of adventure to write your own Indiana Jones screenplay. So, dust off your magnifying glass, polish those coins, and let's turn this daunting journey into a rewarding (and possibly hilarious) escapade.

Selling Strategies

Know Your Audience:

Understanding your audience is paramount in the realm of coin selling, where diverse collectors and investors are driven by various interests and motivations. Tailoring your approach to cater to these distinct groups can significantly enhance your selling success. Here are key considerations and strategies for knowing and engaging your audience effectively:

Identifying Your Audience

Collectors vs. Investors: Recognize the primary motivations of your potential buyers. Collectors often seek coins with historical significance, rarity, or specific attributes that complete or complement their collections. Investors, on the other hand, may prioritize coins based on their metal content, potential for appreciation, or market demand.

Niche Collectors: Within the broader category of collectors, there are niche segments focused on particular types of coins, such as ancient coins, error coins, or coins from a specific country or era. Identifying these niches can help you target your marketing efforts more precisely.

Beginners vs. Experienced Collectors: The level of knowledge and experience can vary widely among collectors. Beginners might need more information and reassurance, while experienced collectors will appreciate detailed specifications and nuanced historical context.

Tailoring Your Approach

Customize Your Communication: When engaging with potential buyers, adjust your language and information based on their level of expertise and interest. Use layman's terms for beginners but be ready to delve into the minutiae for seasoned collectors or knowledgeable investors.

Highlight Relevant Features: Emphasize aspects of the coin that are most likely to appeal to your audience. For collectors, detail the coin's history, rarity, and condition.

For investors, focus on the investment potential, metal content, and market trends affecting its value.

Utilize Appropriate Platforms: Choose selling platforms that align with your target audience. Online marketplaces like eBay or Etsy might be more suitable for a general audience, while specialized forums or auction houses can attract serious collectors and investors. Social media platforms can also be tailored to different groups, with Instagram appealing to a visually oriented audience and Facebook groups catering to specific collecting interests.

Offer Comprehensive Information: Provide thorough descriptions and high-quality images, ensuring that potential buyers have all the information they need to make an informed decision. This builds trust and can be particularly important for online sales where physical inspection isn't possible.

Engage with the Community: Participate in numismatic forums, social media groups, and coin shows to understand your audience better and build relationships. This engagement not only helps you stay informed about market trends and collector interests but also establishes you as a knowledgeable and reliable seller.

Knowing your audience is not just about making a sale; it's about creating a connection that respects and aligns with the buyer's passion for numismatics. By understanding the diverse motivations and preferences of collectors and investors, you can tailor your selling strategy to meet their needs, fostering lasting relationships and ensuring mutual satisfaction in the coin collecting journey.

Pricing It Right

Pricing your coins correctly is crucial in attracting the right buyers and ensuring a fair transaction. Whether you're dealing with bullion or rare numismatic pieces, setting an appropriate price involves balancing market value, buyer expectations, and your own goals. Here's how to navigate the complexities of pricing your coins:

Understanding Market Value

1. Research Recent Sales: Look at auction results, online marketplaces, and dealer sales to gauge the going rate for coins similar to yours. Websites like eBay, Heritage Auctions, and other numismatic platforms can offer a wealth of recent sales data.

2. Utilize Price Guides: Price guides, such as the "Red Book" for U.S. coins or the "Standard Catalog of World Coins" for international pieces, provide benchmark values. Remember, these guides offer a general idea; actual market prices can fluctuate.

3. Consider the Coin's Condition: The condition or grade of a coin dramatically affects its value. Use grading standards from reputable services like NGC or PCGS as references. If possible, getting your coin professionally graded can provide a more objective basis for pricing.

Factors Influencing Price

1. Rarity: The rarer a coin, the higher its potential value. Research the mintage numbers and known populations of your coin to understand its rarity.

2. Demand: A coin's desirability among collectors can significantly impact its price. Some coins may carry historical or artistic significance that boosts their appeal.

3. Metal Content: For bullion coins, the current spot price of the metal (gold, silver, platinum, etc.) will be a key pricing component. However, numismatic value can far exceed metal value for rare or sought-after pieces.

4. Market Conditions: The broader economic environment can influence coin prices, with precious metals often seen as safe havens during economic uncertainty.

Setting the Price

1. Be Realistic: Based on your research, set a price that's competitive yet fair. Overpricing can deter potential buyers, while underpricing may result in lost revenue.

2. Consider Your Selling Platform: Different platforms may command different price expectations. For example, direct sales to collectors might yield higher prices than selling through auctions or dealers, who take a cut.

3. Be Flexible: Be prepared to negotiate with buyers, especially if selling privately. Having a clear understanding of your lowest acceptable price before negotiations start can help you make informed decisions.

4. Update Your Pricing: If your coin doesn't sell, revisit your price in light of any new market information or feedback from potential buyers. The numismatic market is dynamic, and prices can change.

Pricing your coins right is a nuanced process that requires doing your homework and staying attuned to the numismatic market's pulse. By carefully considering all factors that affect a coin's value and being open to adjustment, you can set prices that are attractive to buyers and reflective of your coins' worth. Remember, successful selling is not just about the immediate transaction; it's about building trust and reputation within the numismatic community, which starts with fair and transparent pricing.

Optimize Your Listings

Optimizing your listings is essential in the competitive coin selling market. A well-crafted listing not only attracts more potential buyers but also conveys the value and uniqueness of your coin, setting the stage for a successful sale. Here are strategies to make your listings stand out:

High-Quality Photos

1. Clear, Detailed Images: Use a high-resolution camera to capture clear, detailed images of your coin. Include shots from multiple angles, and highlight any unique features or conditions that affect the coin's value.

2. Natural Lighting: Photograph your coins in natural, soft lighting to avoid glare and shadows. This can help in accurately representing the coin's condition and details.

3. Use a Neutral Background: A plain, neutral background focuses attention on the coin, avoiding distractions and making the details pop.

Compelling Descriptions

1. Be Detailed and Accurate: Provide a thorough description that includes the coin's denomination, year, mint mark, grading information, and any historical or rarity details. Accuracy is key to building buyer trust.

2. Highlight Key Selling Points: Mention what makes your coin special. Is it a rare find? Does it have historical significance? Is it in exceptional condition? Make these features the focal point of your description.

3. Use Keywords Wisely: Incorporate relevant keywords that potential buyers might use in their search queries. This can improve the visibility of your listing in search results.

Pricing and Policies

1. Competitive Pricing: Set a competitive price based on your research of the market and similar listings. Consider including the rationale for your pricing in the description if it adds value and transparency.

2. Clear Payment and Shipping Information: Outline your accepted payment methods, return policy, shipping charges, and any insurance options. Clear policies reduce buyer uncertainty and can prevent disputes.

Engage and Build Trust

1. Encourage Questions: Invite potential buyers to ask questions. This engagement can build trust and provide an opportunity to share more details about the coin.

2. Respond Promptly: Quick responses to inquiries show that you are attentive and reliable, qualities that buyers appreciate in a seller.

3. Share Your Expertise: If you have expertise or special knowledge about the type of coin you're selling, share it in the listing. This can add value to your coin and make your listing more compelling.

Utilize the Platform's Features

1. Use All Available Tools: Take advantage of any tools or features the platform offers, such as video uploads, to give buyers a better look at the coin.

2. Optimize for Mobile: Many buyers shop on their mobile devices. Ensure your listing looks good and reads well on smaller screens.

An optimized listing is your best tool to attract buyers and sell your coin at the desired price. By focusing on high-quality photos, compelling and accurate descriptions, and clear policies, you can set your listing apart in the crowded marketplace. Engaging with potential buyers and leveraging the platform's features can further enhance your listing's visibility and appeal, leading to a successful sale. Remember, each listing is not just about selling a coin; it's about telling its story and connecting with someone who values it as much as you do.

Selling Tips

Build Relationships

In the world of coin selling, establishing and nurturing relationships is as valuable as the coins themselves. Building strong connections with buyers, fellow sellers, and enthusiasts can open doors to opportunities that go beyond a single transaction. Here are strategies to foster these essential relationships:

Engage with the Community

1. Participate in Forums and Social Media: Active participation in numismatic forums, Facebook groups, and Instagram can help you connect with like-minded individuals. Share your knowledge, ask questions, and contribute positively to discussions.

2. Attend Coin Shows and Events: Coin shows are not just venues for buying and selling but also for meeting people with shared interests. Face-to-face interactions can lead to lasting relationships and potential future transactions.

Provide Excellent Customer Service

1. Be Transparent and Honest: Transparency about the condition, authenticity, and history of your coins builds trust. Always disclose any known issues or defects to avoid misunderstandings and maintain your reputation.

2. Respond Promptly and Courteously: Whether you're dealing with inquiries, offers, or after-sales service, timely and respectful communication is key to positive relationships.

Share Your Passion and Knowledge

1. Educate Your Buyers: Many collectors appreciate learning more about their purchases. Sharing interesting facts or the historical significance of a coin can enhance the buying experience and establish you as a knowledgeable seller.

2. Offer Guidance to New Collectors: Helping beginners navigate the complexities of coin collecting can foster goodwill and loyalty. Offer advice on starting a collection, caring for coins, and other basics.

Network with Fellow Sellers

1. Collaborate Rather Than Compete: View fellow sellers as potential collaborators. Sharing leads, exchanging information on buyers, and even joint ventures for coin shows can be mutually beneficial.

2. Learn from Others: More experienced sellers can offer valuable insights into market trends, pricing strategies, and selling platforms. Be open to advice and constructive feedback.

Follow Up and Stay Connected

1. Keep in Touch: After a sale, a simple follow-up to ensure satisfaction can leave a lasting positive impression. Periodic check-ins or newsletters about new acquisitions might encourage repeat business.

2. Utilize Social Media: Regular updates on your social media platforms can keep your network engaged and informed about your offerings and activities.

Building relationships in the coin selling world is about much more than just making sales. It's about creating a network of trust, respect, and shared passion for numismatics. By actively engaging with both the collector and seller communities, providing excellent customer service, and sharing your knowledge and enthusiasm, you can establish a strong foundation for sustained success and fulfillment in the numismatic market.

Utilize Social Media

In the digital age, leveraging social media is not just an option for coin sellers; it's a necessity. Platforms like Instagram, TikTok, and Facebook offer unparalleled opportunities to showcase your coins, connect with collectors, and ultimately drive sales. CoinHub, for instance, serves as an exemplary model of how effectively utilizing social media can turn a passion for numismatics into a thriving business.

Showcasing Coins on Instagram

Instagram's visual-centric platform is ideal for highlighting the beauty and uniqueness of coins. CoinHub utilizes Instagram (@coinhubs) to post high-quality images and videos of coins, sharing detailed captions that provide historical context or interesting facts. This approach not only attracts coin enthusiasts but also educates followers, creating a community of informed collectors. By visiting CoinHub's Instagram, you can see firsthand the power of engaging content and how it fosters a connection with the audience.

Live Streaming for Personal Interaction

Live streaming on platforms like TikTok and Instagram has revolutionized the way sellers interact with potential buyers. CoinHub leverages live streaming to personally connect with followers, offering real-time insights, answering questions, and showcasing coins up close. This direct interaction builds trust and rapport, making followers more likely to consider purchasing from you. Live sessions also allow you to demonstrate your expertise and passion, further establishing your credibility in the numismatic community.

Educating New Collectors

A significant part of CoinHub's social media strategy involves educating new collectors. Through informative posts and live Q&A sessions, newcomers to the hobby can learn about coin collecting basics, grading standards, and investment tips. This educational approach not only nurtures future collectors but also positions CoinHub as a trusted source in the numismatic market. At the end of educational videos, CoinHub seamlessly introduces how followers can start their own collections by purchasing through their platform, effectively turning viewers into customers.

Driving Sales Through Social Media

Utilizing social media for sales involves a delicate balance of showcasing, educating, and engaging. CoinHub demonstrates that by providing value to your followers—whether through fascinating coin facts, market insights, or personal interactions—you can naturally lead them to your sales channels. The key is to maintain a focus on building relationships and offering genuine value, rather than overtly pushing sales. When followers trust and value your content, they're more likely to become loyal customers.

Social media is a powerful tool for coin sellers, offering a platform to showcase coins, interact with followers, and educate new collectors. By following CoinHub's example, you can effectively use social media to build your brand, connect with a dedicated community of coin enthusiasts, and drive sales. Remember, success on social media comes from authentic engagement and providing real value to your audience. Check out CoinHub on Instagram (@coinhubs) and TikTok (@coinhub) to see how it's done, and consider how you can apply these strategies to your own selling efforts.

Shipping Your Coins

Shipping your coins with care and promptness is crucial in maintaining a good reputation as a seller and ensuring customer satisfaction. Here are key strategies to ensure your coins reach their new owners safely and swiftly:

Packaging Coins Securely

1. Use Protective Materials: Coins should be placed in protective flips or capsules to prevent scratches and damage. For extra protection, especially for higher-value items, consider using bubble wrap or foam inserts.

2. Sturdy Shipping Containers: Use rigid, high-quality shipping boxes or padded envelopes that can withstand the rigors of transit. Avoid containers that are too large, as coins can shift during shipping; however, make sure there's enough room for adequate protective padding.

3. Seal and Label Clearly: Securely seal your package using strong tape and label it clearly with the recipient's address. Double-check the address for accuracy to avoid delays. Include a return address in case of delivery issues.

Choosing the Right Shipping Service

1. Consider Delivery Speed: Offering various shipping options lets customers choose how quickly they receive their items. While faster shipping can be more expensive, it often enhances customer satisfaction and encourages repeat business.

2. Tracking and Insurance: Always use shipping services that offer tracking and insurance, particularly for valuable coins. This not only protects you against loss or damage but also provides peace of mind to your customers. Share the tracking number with the buyer as soon as the item is dispatched.

3. Cost-Efficiency: While ensuring coin safety and speedy delivery is paramount, be mindful of shipping costs. Research and compare different carriers and services to find the best balance between cost, reliability, and speed.

Communicating with Your Buyer

1. Confirm Shipping Details: Before dispatching, confirm the shipping address with your buyer. This simple step can prevent misunderstandings and ensure the package is headed to the correct destination.

2. Provide Updates: Notify your buyer once the item has shipped and provide them with the tracking information. Keeping the buyer informed at every step fosters trust and reduces anxiety about the purchase.

3. Follow Up: After the expected delivery date, reach out to your buyer to confirm receipt of the package and ensure their satisfaction with the condition of the coin. This follow-up can go a long way in building a positive seller-buyer relationship.

Why Speed and Care Matter

Fast and careful shipping is more than a logistical necessity; it's a reflection of your commitment to customer service. Buyers remember the excitement of receiving a new coin and the care taken in its presentation and delivery. By prioritizing secure packaging and prompt shipping, you not only protect your coins but also enhance the unboxing experience for your customers, encouraging loyalty and positive reviews.

Shipping with care and speed is essential in the coin selling process. By investing in secure packaging, choosing reliable shipping services, and maintaining clear communication with your buyers, you create a professional and positive buying experience. This attention to detail not only safeguards the coins during transit but also reinforces your reputation as a dependable and considerate seller.

Coin Marketing Summed Up

And there we have it, folks—the grand finale of Chapter 6, where we've journeyed through the wilds of coin selling with the finesse of a numismatic ninja. From mastering the ancient art of "Know Thy Buyer" to the delicate dance of pricing that would make even Goldilocks nod in approval ("Not too high, not too low, just right!"), we've covered the A-Z of turning those shiny discs into shiny profits.

Imagine your coins are like little celebrities, each with its own fan base, backstory, and diva demands. Your job? Being the world's best talent manager. You've got to showcase them in the best light, on the right stage (hello, optimized listings), and make sure their fans (aka buyers) can't resist their charm. And let's not forget about giving them a proper send-off when they leave for their new home—packaging them with care because, let's face it, no one likes receiving a superstar in a crumpled envelope.

Enter CoinHub, the Beyoncé of the numismatic world—a shining example of what happens when passion does the cha-cha with strategy. This platform is like the cool, savvy mentor that shows you how to blend educational content with slick sales tactics, turning every tweet, post, or TikTok into a potential gold mine.

But remember, grasshopper, this chapter is more than a mere blueprint; it's your numismatic dojo. It's about embracing the continuous hustle of learning, the thrill of the hunt for knowledge, and the joy of spreading your coin-collecting enthusiasm like confetti at a parade.

As you march forth with these strategies, clutching your coins and dreams alike, remember that selling isn't just about the cha-ching of the cash register. It's about the tales you tell, the wisdom you weave into each sale, and the friendships you form over shared obsessions with old bits of metal.

So, wear your coin-collecting heart on your sleeve and venture into the marketplace with the courage of a lion and the wisdom of a sage. The numismatic landscape is your playground, and with these tips in your treasure chest, you're not just ready to play the game—you're ready to redefine it.

Let Chapter 6 be not just your guide but also your muse, sparking innovation and curiosity as you carve out your niche in the ever-shifting sands of the coin world. Here's to your success, your discoveries, and, most importantly, to the endless adventure that is numismatics. May your selling journey be as rich and rewarding as the coins you cherish. Onwards and upwards, fellow numismatists!

CHAPTER 7: BEYOND THE COINHUB

Additional Insight from Experts in the Industry

For the final chapter of our book, I reached out to some trusted friends from the Numismatic community to contribute their expertise on topics I'm less familiar with. These areas include selling antique coins and conducting transactions directly with coin shops. While I don't own a physical coin shop and conduct all our sales online, I felt it was essential to get insights from those with firsthand experience. Thus, I invited Evan Kail, who also goes by PawnMan and owns a Minnesota-based pawn shop, to share his knowledge. Additionally, I asked Christian Hartch, founder of the popular YouTube channel Treasure Town with 160,000 subscribers, to provide his perspective on selling ancient coins—an area I'm interested in but have yet to explore personally. With Evan's substantial following of nearly 2 million across social media, and both being influential young numismatists in the industry, their contributions add significant value and depth to the concluding section of our book.

Coins Through Time: My Journey into the World of Ancient and Global Numismatics

By Christian Hartch, Founder of TreasureTown *(160K+ YouTube Subscribers)*

When reflecting on my experience of selling ancient, medieval, and world coins more generally, I've realized how fascinating that journey has been—and how a few unexpected twists and turns led to me becoming such an enthusiast for the material. After Blake reached out to me to discuss some of my thoughts, I figured I would share 5 takeaways and pieces of helpful perspective, along with 5 ideas for new collections that particularly stood out.

1. Coming from the viewpoint of a United States-only coin collector, the sheer amount of learning that collecting world and ancient coins enables is amazing. I initially ventured in with an issuing entity type set—more on that later—focusing on coins minted after the 1800s. There are so many provinces, small countries, and transitional governments that have minted coins, and even being aware of them led to countless Wikipedia searches that bolstered my understanding of world history immensely. And that's not even considering all of the coins minted before the 19th century! From the Greeks and Romans to ancient India and China, to vast Islamic and Mongol empires, to the many additional civilizations over the past few millennia, there is countless history and numismatics to learn—I sure have a long way to go myself.

2. Ever since the 7th century BC, when coinage was invented, inflation has always been an issue for world civilizations and is visible

on the coins they used—it's really fascinating! This is particularly visible on the coins of the Roman Empire in the 3rd century AD, when the "denarius" denomination was replaced by the "antoninianus," which was supposed to have double the face value of the denarius. Of course, it didn't weigh twice as much, and while the government was able to use that to fund spending, later that century, the coins would have silver contents in the single-digit percentage range as opposed to the full silver issues of previous times. The Empire had major issues as a result.

3. Much of the history we know today is derived from coins. For example, I wrote a college paper on how gold coins of the early 5th century ended up in Scandinavia—and the conclusion was that there was either an active fur trade or there were mercenaries that were being paid by or with the loot from the weakening Roman emperors. Rulers exerted their influence and asserted their power by striking coins with it, and while we'd know about the big ones anyway, the smaller ones that tried insurrections (and sometimes were successful!) are also commemorated by the coins they struck. America broke the trend of having kings on their coins with the different designs of Liberty on the coins—as opposed to presidents—and now we only authorize deceased presidents to appear on our coinage.

4. Coins weren't always accepted at their full-face value, and certainly didn't have acceptance across the world... that is also true for American coins, though! That led to much more friction in commerce, which really hurt it—imagine taking

your group of random-sized copper coins to a grocery market and trying to bargain with those! Nobody would know what they should really be worth. And a gold coin would be so valuable that most of the items you'd be paying for would be worth fractions of the face value of the gold. One solution was to literally cut the coins into halves, quarters, or even eighths... other times transactions just wouldn't happen.

5. Many ancient and world coins are shockingly inexpensive, especially relative to their American counterparts. I frequently sell NGC-holdered Widow's Mites of the 2nd-1st Century BC from Ancient Judaea (thought to be referenced in the Bible) at prices under $30 or $35. Many worn coins of the Roman Empire can be acquired, fully identified, for between $8 and $15. So many coins were struck, and not always accepted in commerce as inflation and ruler changes occurred rapidly, so many of them ended up nicely preserved in hoards for two thousand years. That means they remain very accessible to collectors around the world today. And of course, for the larger-budget collectors, there are plenty of pricey items to go around.

Five collections I'd recommend:

1. **Issuing entity type set**—this can be defined in many ways... perhaps dating back to 1800 with no constraints, perhaps all of the United Nations-recognized countries, perhaps some arbitrary timeframe and criteria... but the goal is to collect one coin from every entity that could have produced a coin.

2. **Ruler type set**—this is a great one for a civilization you are particularly interested in... the Roman Empire is a popular one. Start with some of the later 3rd century AD rulers, such as Gallienus, Aurelian, Diocletian, and also check out the 4th century AD types like Constantine the Great, his relatives, and Theodosius the Great. There are plenty of challenging-to-find rulers to make things complicated. Bonus tip: if you want a cheap silver coin, check out Antoninianus of Gordian III.

3. **Zoo**—there are fascinating reverse types that different emperors and rulers struck. Some of the famous types are eagles and owls, but there's everything from hippocampi to stags to bees, lions, boars, turtles, and fish. Collect different animals!

4. **"Box of 20"**—originating from a type of collection I'd heard about elsewhere, the number of coins that fit in a PCGS/NGC coin box is 20. Many more ancient coins are raw versus graded, so it doesn't have to be a box, but limit your collection to 20 coins, and pick the nicest coins you can find (making upgrades along the way). That way, things don't get out of hand, and you'll be forced to be a decent seller in addition to a buyer—and won't go way too fast in accumulating a collection of coins you end up not being as interested in. Of course, it can then be fun to expand the size to 50, 100, 500—you name it. But it's an idea for the budget- (or physical size-) minded numismatist.

5. **Ancestry set**—trace your ancestry as far back as you can, and then purchase coins from those eras! I'm a US-German citizen with relatives from across Europe dating back to the

1300s-1700s, so acquiring some pieces of the countries that my ancestors might have held is exciting to me. You never know who touched a coin before it got lost and dug up years later... remember that almost all ancient coins have been uncovered from digs, metal detectorist efforts, and archaeology!"

TREAD LIGHTLY IN THE MODERN WILD WEST

Evan Kail aka "Pawn Man"

Sharks are apex predators renowned for their acute sense of smell, able to detect a single drop of blood in the water from miles away. In a similar vein, precious metal and coin shop owners share this keen perception, but instead of blood, their radar tunes into the presence of a novice entering their domain. For the uninitiated, the moment you step into one of these businesses, you're like a stab victim plunging into shark-infested waters.

I struggled to hide my glee as I examined a rare collection of uncirculated Morgan Silver Dollars. Had the customer recognized their true value, the situation might have gone differently. Unfortunately for her, I detected a wounded seal that didn't even know how to swim.

My initial impression of the woman, with her distinct bob haircut and designer-style glasses, wasn't entirely positive. She loudly snapped her chewing gum as she spoke to me with an arrogant tone. Yet, as we negotiated, I grew to appreciate her company. This woman, seemingly in her forties and navigating life post-divorce, became more likable as the transaction unfolded. Transactions like these, often involving the exchange of cherished family heirlooms, are a unique aspect of my profession. It's a peculiar line of work, one that requires a period of adjustment. Since entering the business in 2019, I've acquired several strategies to navigate these delicate dealings effectively, a few of which I was currently utilizing.

Our shared laughter echoed in the shop as I slapped a price tag on a stack of silver bullion. I was buying 93 ounces, just a pinch below market value. Already the deal was going to generate a few hundred dollars in profit. Then she showed me the Morgans and uttered the fatal words: "I don't know what I have here, and I don't care what I get."

In that moment, she had inadvertently made herself an easy target in a game of precision and strategy. This encapsulates the essence of my profession: navigating a landscape filled with high stakes and the potential for significant rewards. This is a business where you can make a killing or be killed just as easily. Each one of these deals requires strategy, and a single grave mistake can ruin someone.

In this industry, it's common sense to assume everyone walking through the door is trying to rip you off, or worse. It's important to be a tough negotiator and take advantage of any situation that presents itself during a deal. In this case, the woman wasn't dangerous, but she had given me an opportunity to maximize profits, and sharks who can't swim or eat are eaten by something more cunning.

I proposed the woman $20 for each Morgan, an offer she accepted with delight. I would go on to sell those coins for $200 apiece. Now before you throw this out of your hands screaming what a bad person I am, know that the shop owner down the street would have offered her $17 each, and the one beyond $10, or less. I don't know any sharks that don't devour meals with utter savagery. In the Twin Cities, where I'm based, the remnants of defunct bullion shops serve as a stark reminder. Many of these businesses met their end through acts of kindness that ultimately led to their downfall. All the woman had to do was a tiny bit of research on what she was selling, and I would have offered a lot more money.

The woman pulled out of the parking lot, and soon after, another customer arrived. His presence was a stark contrast. He reeked of cigarettes and body odor, a toxic combination that stabbed my nostrils. He quietly mumbled that he had some gold to sell.

We sat down at my stately oak desk, and I leaned forward to shut off my camera for recording deals, which I upload to social media. The fancy desk itself was a tactical purchase.

Just as I began to question whether I should have offered the woman a bit more, a new figure appeared. The strong odor of cigarettes and body odor filled the air, an unpleasant assault on my senses. He quietly mentioned he had some gold to sell.

We took our seats at my impressive oak desk, where I discreetly turned off my camera. The desk, along with the high-quality office chairs and the ambiance I cultivated, served as another strategic tool in my arsenal for negotiations.

As we sat down, something about him made me feel uneasy. It wasn't just his poor hygiene or unfriendly attitude. He was presenting himself as a careless slob, yet his eyes were like a predator's and his movements suggested he was dead sober. To me, it indicated this wasn't his first rodeo; he wasn't a fool, he was just dressed up as one.

"Let's see what you have to sell," I said.

He presented a gleaming 18kt gold chain, which raised the first of several red flags. By my experience, men's 18kt gold chains and bracelets are the most popular counterfeit item scammers use. This is because the purity is higher than 14kt, and they tend to have a decent amount of weight to them.

His behavior hinted at another red flag: As I began the testing process, his predatory eyes flickered like a snake sensing a bird from above. "What are you doing?" he demanded.

"I need to test this," I explained calmly. "I'll just rub it against this granite stone a bit. It's a standard practice to verify the gold's authenticity. Every shop does this."

His defensiveness escalated. "That's messed up, judging me based on how I look! Are you racist or something?

"I have to verify this gold is legitimate before I buy it. It's a routine check for everyone," I reassured him, trying to defuse the situation.

Noticing he had tensed up, practically hovering inches above his seat, I proceeded with extra caution, aiming to avoid any sudden movements that could escalate tensions. The nature of this business might be unforgiving but armed with a Springfield .45 caliber handgun on my hip, I had no desire for conflict.

Gently, I scratched the chain against a granite block and applied 18kt nitric acid to the mark. I returned the chain to him and waited.

"Looking good so far," I said.

After a tense minute, during which his heavy breathing was the only sound over the air conditioner, he triumphantly declared, "See? One hundred percent real! Told you. Can I get cash for this?"

"Just a moment," I responded.

"But you just said it's good."

"Now I'm saying wait a moment." Maintaining control like this was another skill I'd learned, especially when a situation turned tense.

Slowly, the mark on the granite started to disappear, definitively proving the gold's inauthenticity. This was a good fake, too. Most fakes can't hold up to acid for more than a few seconds. Now I had to politely tell this con artist to take his show on the road elsewhere.

"Sorry, but I can't buy this. If it doesn't pass the acid test, I'm just not comfortable taking it on," I said. Unless I catch someone stealing, I always politely decline a transaction, even if I know for certain they were trying to rip me off.

He argued, as most do, but saw his scam wasn't going to work and left, muttering obscenities under his breath.

I field this sort of unpleasant interaction all the time, and I've built a business showcasing how wild it can be online. If you don't know who I am, I'll give you a quick summary since Blake was so kind to include me in his book.

Before the pandemic struck, I was in search of a new direction. I'd tried and failed to become a writer, sinking my entire 20s into the prospect. Then, quite unexpectedly, a door opened. My father shared that an elderly shopkeeper, in need of an apprentice for his gold and silver shop, was seeking a young person to take over his business.

At the time, it seemed ridiculous. I knew little about precious metals, and even less about numismatics. My father had once been a renowned figure in the coin collecting world, but I hadn't ever considered it. Yet, driven by necessity, I accepted the position. To my surprise, it was a perfect match, almost as if it was meant to be. I fell in love with the industry almost immediately, and within a year, I was inadvertently following in my father's footsteps.

The shop where I began my journey was primarily focused on bullion, scrap metal, rare coins, and currency. However, using online sales tactics, I expanded operations to include collectibles and antiques, adding a new dimension to the business. Eventually, the fascinating day-to-day discoveries propelled me to create a social media presence under the moniker "Pawn Man." The shop I was at disagreed with my strategy, and in 2021, I left to open my own store, St. Louis Park Gold and Silver. Today, with nearly 2 million followers, I've managed to carve out both a prominent personal brand and a thriving business, but I don't just make content about the intense interactions I have with people. I take pride in arming my audience with knowledge about everything from tidbits of history to the realities of the industry. Most people don't know the first thing about it, and that's exactly what predatory shops bank on. It's a wild west shark tank, and whether buying or selling, you should know a few basics to avoid falling prey.

I'm an outlier with my age, as this industry seems to be dominated by older people, and from experience, they can be quite particular. Conduct yourself appropriately from the moment you set foot inside, especially if you plan to visit again. Hygiene is important, especially if you intend to haggle. Bad hygiene to me suggests nothing positive, and I'm personally more likely to reject an offer if the person smells unpleasant. Clean hands are important too. If you're viewing a coin, a shop owner isn't likely to let you touch it if your hands are covered in grime.

It's also important to be conscientious of a person's time. If you're asking for service, know that you're taking up the most valuable thing the business owner has to offer. The owner is likely to treat you better if you're punctual with your time, and especially if you're spending money. If you make a habit of window shopping, don't be surprised if a shop owner isn't friendly.

Only a few individuals are banned from my store, among which include a father and son duo. Their disruptive behavior serves as a prime example; they were not only unpleasant and confrontational but also engaged in persistent lowballing, wasted my time, and were notably lacking in personal hygiene. While it's expected that customers will seek a deal, it's important to approach these discussions with respect and an understanding that the seller's listed price is generally an indication of the value they hope to receive. Approaching negotiations with courtesy significantly enhances the likelihood of a successful transaction and a more positive overall experience.

Despite the seemingly benign nature of a business that deals primarily with coins, it's a surprisingly risky field that demands caution. Keep in mind, shop owners are tangoing with the public at large, many of whom are trying to be deceitful. Always maintain a calm attitude and ensure that your hands are visible when inside a shop. Leave your guns and knives in the car. Avoid taking photos or videos, too. Most shop owners restrict this sort of activity and will get very upset if you infringe upon it. Abrupt movements or any behavior that could be perceived as a potential threat should be keenly avoided. It's a known fact that many shop owners take their security seriously, to the extent of being armed.

The wariness between shop owner and customer is a two-way street. When you're poised to make a purchase, it's critical to employ precautions. People fall for coin scams every day, so do some research about what it is you're buying before you visit a shop, and not just mintage years or basic facts. A well-prepared numismatist is aware of live metal prices, market trends in collectibles, and spotting fraudulent coins. This includes a basic understanding of coin grading, and "Sham grading."

Coin grading has taken over the American collectible coin market, with scores assigned to coins directly correlating to their value. However, when visiting a shop, just because you see a grade written on a coin doesn't mean it's a worthwhile opinion. In the realm of coin grading, there are three organizations I hold in high regard: PCGS, NGC, and ANACS, the latter of which I jokingly refer to as the "ugly red-headed stepchild" of the group. That's because most collectors seem to view PCGS and NGC as the premier authorities who score coins with the most accuracy. For those unfamiliar, coins are evaluated using a 70-point scale known as the Sheldon Grading Scale, introduced in 1949 by Dr. William Sheldon. He chose the 70-point system under the notion that a penny in mint condition would be worth 70 times its face value.

Dr. Sheldon could hardly have anticipated the dramatic expansion of the collector market, where coins now can fetch millions of dollars, but the scale is studied and renowned by numismatists worldwide. The grade of a coin significantly influences its price, and there are professionals who earn their livelihood by purchasing coins, having them graded, and then selling them for a profit. As the owner of a coin shop, I invest thousands annually in grading services, and it's a practice that pays dividends.

Coin grading is often seen as a blend of art and science, heavily reliant on both experience and subjective judgment. Mastering the nuances of this craft demands years of dedicated practice, and even then, interpretations can vary significantly based on how individuals apply the Sheldon Grading Scale. While the grading process has been largely formalized, with comprehensive guidebooks available for most coin types, discrepancies in evaluations can occur, highlighting the subjective element inherent in the practice. Trust only coins graded by NGC, PCGS, ANACS, and avoid anything else. Overgrading is a major scam tactic in numismatics, and consumers should be wary of "sham graders"—fly-by-night operations established solely to perpetrate fraud, issuing baseless grades to subpar coins, encasing them in inferior holders, and selling them to the unwary.

As a concluding piece of advice for buyers, remember to bring cash. Many business owners in this field operate with a traditional mindset, and only accept cash. Be ready to encounter a surcharge or, in some cases, an outright refusal of sale if you intend to pay with a credit card.

It might surprise you to know most people entering my shop aren't buying; rather, they're selling, and if anything, this is the arena people need to be most cautious. By my experience, most shop owners play dirty. I've witnessed a few local shop owners outright lie and say to people their gold wasn't real when they knew it sure was. Such tactics are not only reprehensible but also illegal, yet it's surprisingly common.

It's crucial to understand that even in the most reputable shops, the owner's primary objective isn't to offer you a fair payout. Many people harbor the misconception that they can simply cash in their old coins and collectibles for their full value. In reality, this is a business where the aim is to maximize profit margins, particularly given the high operational costs inherent in this sector. This doesn't mean all shop owners are thieves, but it does underscore the importance of approaching such transactions with caution and well-informed knowledge.

Approach selling as if it were a strategic game of poker, with all knives out. As mentioned earlier, never reveal ignorance about what you possess, nor express indifference about the compensation you receive. Doing so is akin to showing your cards. Admitting ignorance opens the door for exploitation and disclosing you don't care about what you sell for is begging to be lowballed.

From a shop owner's perspective, it's not cruelty but logical; why forgo significant profit due to someone's lack of research? Before selling, learn your item's value and consider obtaining multiple quotes to ensure you're receiving a fair offer. Remember, there's no harm in telling a shop owner you'll need time to think it over before deciding. Know the metals market the day you intend to sell and ask yourself if the offer is fair market value, or if it's pennies on the dollar? There is a free app I recommend called KITCO to track live metal prices.

Once you've done your homework and know the value of your items, it's wise to have a target price in mind before you start negotiating, particularly if you're dealing with a substantial collection. This approach not only benchmarks the fairness of the offer you receive against the market value but also deters potential exploitation. It signals to the buyer that you are informed and respect their time, which can influence the negotiation positively. Presenting a price upfront is a strategy rarely employed by sellers, yet it can lead to more straightforward transactions. I've noticed that, faced with a significant volume of items, a seller who demonstrates awareness of their value can prevent shop owners from resorting to quick, undervalued estimations to save time and increase profit margins.

Additionally, if you're selling and a shop owner tells you your items aren't real, ask them to prove it. Virtually all these shops possess testing equipment. Should you catch a seller being dishonest, it's advisable to get up and leave. Neglectful integrity in one arena often reflects broader deceitfulness.

Just like as a consumer, when selling, it's good to maintain good hygiene and polite manners. If the offer doesn't meet your expectations, a simple "No, thank you" suffices. Remember, as the saying goes, "You catch more bees with honey than vinegar." Since the shop owner is the one writing the check, any perceived disrespect could literally cost you.

Finally, digest your own situation and be prepared to relinquish things readily. The shop owner didn't place you in this situation, nor are they obligated to compensate for family nostalgia. They've never met your long-deceased great-grandmother, nor did they advise you to rack up all that gambling debt. That you must sell her silverware set is of no concern to them. They're providing you with a potential solution to your cash shortage and bringing personal reluctance into a transaction only serves to sour the interaction.

Regardless of whether you're on the buying or selling side, navigating this industry is akin to swimming in treacherous waters teeming with sharks eager for an effortless feast. Safeguarding yourself isn't challenging, especially since many shops target what they perceive as vulnerable individuals. By heeding the advice I've shared, you can protect yourself effectively. Craft a baseball bat of knowledge and beat back anyone trying to prey on you. Engaging with your local coin shop can result in a fruitful business relationship and offer valuable learning opportunities. Just remember to walk lightly and carry a big stick.

ENHANCE YOUR COIN COLLECTING EXPERIENCE WITH COINHUB

At CoinHub, we've combined our passion for numismatics with the latest technology to provide an engaging, interactive auction experience on Whatnot. Our commitment to the coin collecting community is evident not only in our content but also in the exciting opportunities we offer to both new and returning members of our vibrant community.

Exclusive Offers for The CoinHub Readers

First-Time Buyers: To welcome new members to our CoinHub family, we're thrilled to offer a $15 gift card to all new buyers. Simply use the code "COINHUB" at our Whatnot store (coinhubstore.com) during your first purchase to claim your gift. It's our way of saying thank you for joining us on this numismatic journey.

Returning Buyers: We value our community and appreciate every member who chooses to engage with us repeatedly. As a token of our gratitude for buying this book, returning buyers can use the code "THECOINHUBBOOK" to receive a $3 discount on their next order. This ongoing engagement is what strengthens our community and enriches the collecting experience.

How to Participate in Our Live Streams

CoinHub's live streams on Whatnot are designed to cater to collectors worldwide, offering flexibility and an exciting platform to enhance your collecting experience. Whether you prefer the calm of the evening or the fresh start of the morning, our streaming schedule is tailored to suit various lifestyles:

Evening Streams: Join us every Monday, Thursday, and Saturday at 8 PM EST. Perfect for unwinding after a day's work, these sessions dive deep into the world of coins, offering insights and opportunities to add to your collection.

Morning Streams: Kick off your Friday mornings at 11 AM EST with CoinHub. These streams are great for starting your day with a dose of numismatics, engaging with the community, and participating in live auctions.

Exciting Giveaways During Our Streams

During each live stream, we don't just auction off coins; we also host giveaways! These are fantastic opportunities for participants to win exceptional coins simply by being part of our live audience. It adds an extra thrill to the live auction experience and offers more ways to engage with our community.

Join Our Community

To join our streams and start participating in auctions or giveaways, visit us at **coinhubstore.com**. Here, you can also find our live streaming schedule and keep up with upcoming events. Don't forget to visit our website, coin-hubmedia.com, to download the first book of this series for free and dive deeper into the art of coin collecting.

CoinHub is not just a platform; it's a gateway to a world where the love for coins bridges past and present, merging tradition with modern technology. Whether you're here to grow your collection, learn more about numismatics, or simply enjoy the community atmosphere, CoinHub welcomes you to be part of a journey that celebrates the art and history of coins in a contemporary, dynamic way. Join us for our next stream, and let's explore the fascinating world of coin collecting together!

ABOUT THE AUTHOR

Blake Alma is an entrepreneur and author whose passion for coins and precious metals sparked a journey into the numismatic world. From his modest beginnings as a young enthusiast, Blake has evolved into a prominent figure in the coin collecting community, founding CoinHub Media and authoring the best-selling book, "The CoinHub: An Ultimate Guide to Coin Errors."

Growing up with an inherent fascination for the intricate details and storied past of coins, Blake's initial interest in numismatics blossomed into a career path that seamlessly blended his hobbies with his professional aspirations. His straightforward writing style, peppered with a touch of humor, has endeared him to readers and followers alike, making complex subjects accessible and engaging.

In January 2020, Blake launched CoinHub, initially as a blog and a platform on social media channels like TikTok and Instagram. This venture quickly gained traction, amassing a large following that resonated with Blake's infectious enthusiasm and expert insights into modern U.S. coin errors and their values. His content not only educates but also builds a community among collectors, both seasoned and new.

Blake's success was not just limited to social media; it also translated into significant achievements on newer platforms like Whatnot, where live streaming allowed him to interact personally with followers, enhancing engagement and driving sales. Through live sessions, Blake educates his audience, sharing tips on how to start their own collections and where to make purchases, primarily directing them to CoinHub.

Now residing in Lebanon, Ohio, Blake continues his education, pursuing a degree in marketing at Pensacola Christian College. This academic pursuit complements his career, equipping him with advanced marketing knowledge to further enhance his business endeavors. Despite his busy schedule, Blake still finds time to indulge in his love for the great outdoors, particularly enjoying fishing—a nod to his simpler pleasures.

Recognized for his contributions to the numismatic industry, including features in prestigious publications like the New York Post and Fox Business, Blake remains humble. He credits his success to the supportive coin collecting community and his strong Christian faith, which guides him through all aspects of his life.

Blake Alma's journey from a coin enthusiast to a respected figure in the coin collecting world exemplifies how passion, when coupled with determination and continuous learning, can lead to remarkable achievements. Through CoinHub Media, Blake continues to serve and inspire the coin collecting community, fostering a sense of connection and shared passion among collectors worldwide. He looks forward to continuing his journey in the fascinating realm of coin collecting, always striving to learn, grow, and contribute more to this captivating field.

Made in the USA
Las Vegas, NV
09 May 2024